SEARCHING
ISSUES

7

SEARCHING ISSUES

NICKY
GUMBEL

Published in North America by Alpha North America, 2275 Half Day Road, Suite 185, Deerfield, IL 60015

© 2013 by Nicky Gumbel

This edition issued by special arrangement with Alpha International, Holy Trinity Brompton, Brompton Road, London SW7 1JA, UK

Searching Issues
by Nicky Gumbel

Originally published by KINGSWAY COMMUNICATIONS LTD, Lottbridge Drove, Eastbourne, BN23 6NT, England

First printed by Alpha North America in 2013

Printed in the United States of America

Illustrations by Charlie Mackesy

ISBN 978-1-938328-43-5

1 2 3 4 5 6 7 8 9 10 Printing/Year 16 15 14 13

CONTENTS

PREFACE

There is currently an explosion of interest in spiritual matters. It is difficult to get away from TV programs, online discussion, and newspaper articles concerned with the search for meaning and purpose, life after death, and the existence of God. Among these, many are taking a new look at Christianity. Several television series, such as *The Big Silence* and *The Monastery*, followed ordinary people with almost no familiarity with Catholicism or the monastic living alongside the monks of Worth Abbey, a Benedictine monastery in West Sussex, England. The program generated extraordinary interest. Similar shows have since appeared in the USA and in Australia.

While discussing the Christian faith, especially with those who are not Christians, I have found that a number of questions are raised time and again. Some of these questions are about the place of Christianity in today's world. For example, how does Christianity relate to modern science? Or, how might Christians respond to the charge that religion does more harm than good, and has no place in modern society at all? Other questions concern particular problems internal to Christian belief itself, such as how Christianity responds to other faiths, or how it makes sense to believe that God is both One and Three Persons—Father, Son and Holy Spirit.

In Alpha, a course that is designed to be of help to people with such objections, we give talks based on the material in another book, *Questions of Life*. It is often in the discussion groups afterwards that objections are raised. Those in the course may agree with much of what is being said in the talk, but they often say, "What about. . .?" This book is about those "whats." In this book, I want to look at those issues which are usually seen as objections to Christian faith, but which range a bit beyond the approach of *Questions of Life*. They are all "searching issues," both in the sense that they are asked by those searching for the truth and in the sense that they are demanding and difficult to answer.

Today, some would suggest that "faith" is irrational by definition. Despite its vital importance in many people's lives, it is seen to be without evidence and remains immune to criticism. In the last chapter, "Is Faith Irrational?," I address this underlying question directly, and I suggest that there are good reasons to believe, and that being a Christian is no blind or irrational leap. Nevertheless, to claim that Christian faith is not irrational is not the same as saying that everything in the Christian faith can be completely and easily understood. We live in a world full of mysteries, and in that

respect Christianity is no different. This book seeks to deal frankly with important questions and challenges, to respond to some of the great *searching issues* of Christianity.

Faith is a part of life, and this book seeks to be true to that life. Another aspect of being true to life is to acknowledge that a convincing and viable answer to some of the biggest questions in the universe will never be just about the head. Life is also about the heart. Answers to questions should not just be logically adequate: they should change our lives. This book seeks to ask not just how God could permit suffering, but to glimpse the God who is with us in our suffering in a way that transforms our experience. It does not merely try to satisfy our logical brains with an answer about a God who is both Three and One, it seeks to offer this to us as a great mystery that leads us into worship, and that offers a deeper sense not only of who God is, but who we are created to be.

These great *searching issues*, of science and the place of religion in history, of suffering, and of the nature of God, really do lie at the heart of the Christian faith, and our hope is that through reading this you will come to see that the Christian faith—far from being an irrational leap in which you leave your brain behind—is at heart open to a continuing dialogue, to humble self-enquiry. In fact, sometimes it is through our very engagement with these *searching issues* that we can catch a fresh glimpse of the great and mysterious God whom we worship.

Each question is vast and complex. Every one of the issues involves major theological themes. Obviously, not all matters can be dealt with in a few pages. Each chapter is an attempt to summarize some of the main arguments and to suggest practical guidelines.

I would like to thank all those who have helped me with their comments on this new edition, especially the Rev. David Ingall, the Rev. Pete Bellenger, Julia Evans, and Mark Knight. My thanks to Jo Glen, Patricia Hall, Helena Hird, the Rev. Chris Ash, David Sinclair, the Rev. Graham S. Tomlin, Chris Simmonds, Tom Smiley, Tamsen Carter, Philippa Pearson Miles, Jon Soper, and Dr. Roland Werner for their work on the original book.

CHAPTER 1

WHY DOES GOD ALLOW SUFFERING?

A young New Yorker named Glenn Chambers had a lifelong dream to work for God in Ecuador. At the airport on the day of departure, he wanted to send a note to his mother but he didn't have time to buy a card. He noticed a piece of paper on the terminal floor and picked it up. It turned out to be an advertisement with "Why?" spread across it. He scribbled his note around the word "Why?" That night his airplane exploded into the 14,000-foot Colombian peak El Tablazo. When his mother received the note after the news of his death, the question burned up at her from the page . . . "Why?"

The issue of suffering is the most frequently raised objection to the Christian faith. We are constantly confronted by suffering. "The fact of suffering undoubtedly constitutes the single greatest challenge to the Christian faith, and has been in every generation. Its distribution and degree appear to be entirely random and therefore unfair."[1]

First, we see suffering on a global scale, affecting entire nations or communities. Natural disasters, such as earthquakes, famines, and floods, bring pervasive and arbitrary suffering to the world. Besides the two World Wars, which focused attention on global suffering in an acute form, bitter conflicts and terrorism around the world continue to bring great suffering to families and societies. But it is not only war that causes such violence.

Second, we see community tragedies. One of the worst disasters in Britain, which is still leaving its mark over half a century later, was in Aberfan, South Wales, on 21 October 1966, when a huge coal-tip collapsed and devastated Pantglas Junior School, killing one hundred sixteen children and twenty-eight adults. Almost daily we read or hear of a plane crashing, a ship sinking, or some other disaster affecting the lives of hundreds of people.

Third, suffering at an individual level affects us all to a greater or lesser extent. There is the suffering of bereavement, sickness, disability, broken relationships, unhappy marriages, involuntary singleness, depression, loneliness, abject poverty, persecution, rejection, unemployment, injustice, fierce temptation, and disappointment. Suffering can come in an endless variety of forms and no human being is immune to it.

It is worth noting that suffering is not a problem for all religions. It is an acute problem for the Judeo-Christian tradition because the belief is that God is both utterly good and all-powerful. C. S. Lewis stated the opposing argument succinctly: "If God were good, He would wish to make His creatures perfectly happy, and if God were almighty, He would be able to do what He wished. But the creatures are not happy. Therefore, God lacks either goodness, or power, or both."[2]

Theologians and philosophers have wrestled for centuries with the problem of suffering and no one has ever come up with a simple and complete solution. The Bible is primarily a practical book and it never addresses this issue systematically in a philosophical way. What we see are a number of approaches to the problem, all the way through from Genesis to Revelation. There seem to be four main overlapping insights, and we shall look at each of them in turn.

Human freedom

From beginning to end, the Bible tells a story that puts some of our most basic questions as human beings into context. In the beginning, it tells of a world in which there is no evil and no suffering.

Suffering is not part of God's original created order (Genesis 1–2). There was no suffering in the world before humanity rebelled against God. At the end of the story, God redeems the world and ends all suffering. There will be no suffering when God creates "a new heaven and a new earth" (Revelation 21:1). There will be no more crying and no more pain.

Suffering entered the world only because Adam and Eve sinned. It is, therefore, an alien intrusion into God's world. If all suffering is a result of sin, directly or indirectly, why did God allow sin to enter the world?

He did so because He loves us and wanted to give us free will. Love is not love if it is forced; it can only be love if there is a real choice. God gave human beings the choice and the freedom to love or not to love. Given this freedom, men and women from the beginning have chosen to break God's laws and the result has been suffering. Again, as C. S. Lewis puts it:

> It would, no doubt, have been possible for God to remove by miracle the results of the first sin ever committed by a human being; but this would not have been much good unless He was prepared to remove the results of the second sin, and of the third, and so on forever. If the miracles ceased, then sooner or later we might have reached our present lamentable situation: if they did not, then a world, thus continually underpropped and corrected by Divine interference, would have been a world in which nothing important ever depended on human choice, and in which choice itself would soon cease from the certainty that one of the apparent alternatives before you would lead to no results and was therefore not really an alternative.[3]

Precisely because He loves us, God has created us with freedom. Without a doubt, some of the suffering we endure in this life is because of *our own sin*. Through our own selfish and wrong choices we, sadly, harm ourselves. At times, suffering is the inevitable consequence of breaking God's law. There are physical laws of nature: for example, if we put our hand in the fire it gets burned. In this context, pain acts as an early warning system when we exercise wrong choices. There are also moral laws. God made a world built on moral foundations and there is a natural connection between sin and its consequences. If a person abuses drugs, drug addiction may be the consequence. If we drink excessively, we may eventually suffer from alcoholism. If someone drinks and drives a car and is injured, their injuries are partially the result of their sin. In a similar way, selfishness, greed, lust, arrogance, and bad temper often lead to broken relationships and unhappiness of one sort or another.

Sometimes in the Bible God intervenes actively to judge in this life, but it is important to note that in the Bible there is not an automatic link between a specific sin and a specific experience of suffering. The biblical flood is an example of suffering on a global scale caused by sin resulting in God's judgment. When "the Lord saw how great the wickedness of the human race had become on the earth, and that every inclination of the thoughts of their hearts was only evil all the time . . . his heart was filled with pain" (Genesis 6:5-6). In the case of Sodom and Gomorrah, a community disaster was caused by God's judgment of sin. At other times we see God's judgment on an individual's sin (2 Kings 5:27; Luke 1:20; John 5:14; Acts 5:1-11; 1 Corinthians 11:30).

Job's friends thought Job's suffering must be the result of his sin—but they were wrong (Job 42:7-8). Jesus expressly repudiates the automatic link between sin and suffering, in John 9. When His disciples ask, "who sinned, this man or his parents, that he was born blind?," Jesus' response is that "neither this man nor his parents sinned" (9:2). He also points out that natural disasters are not a form of punishment from God, when He asks, "Do you think that these Galileans were worse sinners than all the other Galileans because they suffered this way? I tell you, no!" (Luke 13:1-5). The apostle Peter draws a distinction between suffering as a result of our own sin ("a beating for doing wrong"—1 Peter 2:20) and suffering which has no connection with our sin ("unjust suffering"—v.19) or suffering "for doing good" (v.20). In light of these careful distinctions made by the Bible, it would be wrong to say this or that event or suffering takes place because of some sin that is related to a person, people or region, as a kind of direct judgment from God.

While it may be appropriate for us to examine our own hearts when we are suffering, we need to be very careful about making judgments about why others are suffering. British church leader David Watson, who died of cancer at the age of fifty, pointed out the dangers of making judgments on others:

> The danger about coupling suffering with sin is that the sick person may often feel guilty anyway. Many times I have talked with those who are seriously ill, and I have found them anxiously wondering what they had done to bring about their condition. They blame themselves; or if they cannot live with that, they project their guilt on to others or God. It's someone's fault! The trouble is that either feelings of guilt, which are often imaginary, or direct accusations, which are often unfair, only encourage the sickness. Both hinder healing.
>
> Yet I know how easy this is. Sometimes I have thought of my asthma or cancer as being punishment for sin. I remember with shame many foolish

things I have done in the past, and with a fairly sensitive conscience it is not hard to feel both guilty and condemned. The positive side is that every affliction has caused me to search deeply within my heart and to repent of every sinful action or attitude that I could discover. I have known many people who have been dramatically healed following such repentance together with the experience of God's forgiveness. It is no bad thing, therefore, to consider carefully our life in the sight of God in order to know the joy and freedom of his love.

At the same time, the negative side of all this comes when such heart-searching leads to nagging and unhealthy feelings of guilt, and perhaps to a very poor image of God. Is it conceivable, when we see Jesus healing the sick and forgiving the sinful, that God should say, "Ah, there's David Watson. He slipped up rather badly last month so I'll afflict him with asthma for the next twenty years"? Or later, "He's upset me again, so this time I'll destroy him with cancer"? Such thoughts are not only ridiculous; they are almost blasphemous, and utterly alien to a God of infinite love and mercy as we see him so clearly in Jesus.[4]

Much of the suffering in the world is the result of *other people's sin*. This is true of many global and community disasters. So much suffering is caused by war, which is always the result of human sin, even if the sin is often on both sides. Much of the starvation in the world is caused by the unequal distribution of the world's resources, or by civil war, or some other human sin. Even the Aberfan disaster was not a "natural" one. A five-month enquiry headed by Lord Justice Edmund Davies ruled that the Coal Board was responsible for the disaster. As one woman who contributed to the disaster fund wrote: "I raged against God, but then I realized it had happened because of man's greed and incompetence."[5]

Likewise, individual suffering is often caused by the sin of others. So much suffering is caused by murder, adultery, theft, sexual abuse, unloving parents, reckless, or drunken driving, slander, unkindness, or selfishness of one kind or another. Some have estimated that perhaps as much as 95 percent of the world's suffering can be accounted for in this way.

This leaves a small proportion that can only be explained as being the result of the fact that we live in a fallen world: a world where all creation has been affected by the sin of human beings. It is the result of Adam and Eve's sin that "thorns and thistles" entered the world (Genesis 3:18). Ever since that time "the creation was subjected to frustration" (Romans 8:20). "Natural" disasters are a result of this disorder in creation.

Human freedom does not always answer the question why a particular individual or nation suffers so much but it does help explain the origin of suffering. All suffering is the result of sin, either directly as a result of my own, or of someone else's sin, or indirectly, as a result of living in a fallen world.

God works through suffering

The second insight is that God, because He loves us, uses suffering for good in a number of different ways. He works through suffering. Suffering is not a good in itself, nor is it directly *caused* by God, but God is able to *use* it for good.

First, suffering is used by God to draw us to Christ. C. S. Lewis wrote:

> God whispers to us in our pleasures, speaks in our conscience, but shouts in our pains; it is His megaphone to rouse a deaf world . . . No doubt pain as God's megaphone is a terrible instrument; it may lead to a final and unrepented rebellion. But it gives the only opportunity the bad man can have for amendment. It removes the veil; it plants the flag of truth within the fortress of a rebel soul.[6]

This has proved true time and again in Christian experience. We meet those who have begun to think about God only as a result of suffering the loss of a loved one, a broken relationship or some other pain in their lives.

Second, God can work through our suffering, and use it to bring us to Christian maturity. Even Jesus "learned obedience from what he suffered" (Hebrews 5:8). God can use suffering to build our characters. One image used by the New Testament is that of the discipline of children. The writer of Hebrews says that "our fathers disciplined us for a little while as they thought best; but God disciplines us for our good, that we may share in his holiness" (Hebrews 12:10). He points out that "no discipline seems pleasant at the time, but painful. Later on, however, it produces a harvest of righteousness and peace for those who have been trained by it" (Hebrews 12:11).

Peter uses a completely different image: that of a metal worker refining silver and gold. He writes that his readers may all "have had to suffer grief in all kinds of trials" (1 Peter 1:6). He goes on to explain why God allows this: "These have come so that the proven genuineness of your faith—of greater worth than gold, which perishes even though refined by fire—may result in praise, glory and honor when Jesus Christ is revealed" (1 Peter 1:7).

God also uses suffering to make our lives more fruitful. Jesus, using a different image on a similar theme, said that as a gardener prunes the vine, so God prunes every fruitful branch "so that it will be even more fruitful" (John 15:2).

Any of us, faced with suffering, will at times ask what the purpose of it all is, and where God is to be found within it. Paul tells us that we can be absolutely sure that God is working in our lives through it: "We know that in all things [that means good things and things that are not so good], God works for the good of those who love him, who have been called according to his purpose" (Romans 8:28). This again has proved true, time and again, in Christian experience. The late nineteenth—and early-twentieth-century preacher Smith Wigglesworth, who had a remarkable ministry of healing, said: "Great faith is the product of great fights. Great testimonies are the outcome of great tests. Great triumphs can only come after great trials."'

No one could wish suffering upon themselves or others, and yet there are many testimonies from individuals who have found an intense episode of pain and suffering to be one of the most transformative seasons of their lives. A long-time barrister and now judge, Christopher Compston, wrote:

> Over twenty-three years ago, my first son Harry died after only thirty-six hours. At the time, his death seemed monstrously unfair and, in one sense, it undoubtedly was. Now, with hindsight, I am quite certain his death was one of the best things that has ever happened to me in that it began the process of breaking me down so that, with God's grace, I could begin to understand how other people felt and how other people suffered.[7]

Likewise, witnessing this suffering in the lives of others can sometimes be profoundly moving. David Watson wrote shortly before his death of the power of suffering to make God's work in people's lives all the more evident:

There is no doubt that millions of Christians all down the centuries have become more Christ-like through suffering. I know of many who have an almost ethereal beauty about them, refined through pain. In fact those who have experienced more of the love of God than anyone I have ever met have also endured more suffering. When you crush lavender, you find its full fragrance; when you squeeze an orange, you extract its sweet juice. In the same way it is often through pains and hurts that we develop the fragrance and sweetness of Jesus in our lives. An agnostic Professor of Philosophy at Princeton University became a Christian when he studied carefully the lives of some of the great saints of God throughout the history of the Church. What struck him especially was their radiance in the midst of pain. Often they suffered intensely, far more than most other people, yet through all their agony their spirits shone with a glorious lustre that defied extinction. This philosopher became convinced that some power was at work within them, and this discovery eventually brought him to Christ.[8]

Of course, in all this our temptation would be to say to God, "I'm quite happy as I am. Please leave me alone." But, as C. S. Lewis points out, that would be to want God to love us less.

Over a sketch made idly to amuse a child, an artist may not take much trouble: he may be content to let it go even though it is not exactly as he meant it to be. But over the great picture of his life—the work which he loves, though in a different fashion, as intensely as a man loves a woman or a mother a child—he will take endless trouble—and would, doubtless, thereby give endless trouble to the picture if it were sentient. One can imagine a sentient picture, after being rubbed and scraped and re-commenced for the tenth time, wishing that it were only a thumb-nail sketch whose making was over in a minute. In the same way, it is natural for us to wish that God had designed for us a less glorious and less arduous destiny; but then we are wishing not for more love but for less.[9]

Third, God often uses suffering to bring about His good purposes. We see an example of this in the life of Joseph (Genesis 37-50). He suffered from rejection by his close family, was separated from those he loved and forcibly removed to Egypt, away from his father, whom he did not see again for twenty years. In Egypt, he was unjustly imprisoned for a crime that he did not commit. For thirteen years he faced trials, temptations, and testing until at the age of thirty he was made ruler over Egypt and was put in a position to save the lives of not only his family, but also of all God's people. Towards the end of his life he was able to speak of his suffering to his brothers, saying, "You intended to harm me, but God intended it for good to accomplish what is now being done, the saving of many lives" (Genesis 50:20).

It is not always easy to see at the time what God is doing. Earlier on in his life, Joseph would not have been able to see it so clearly. Often we cannot work out what is going on or why we are suffering in the way we are.

Handley Moule, when he was Bishop of Durham, had the task of visiting the relatives of 170 miners who had been killed in a mining accident. While he was wondering what to say to them, he picked up a little bookmark his mother had given him. As he held it up, on the reverse side of the handwoven bookmark there was a tangled web. There was no rhyme, no reason, no pattern, nothing. But on the other side it said, "God is love." The world may seem a tangled web, but behind it all is the love of God.

We have seen that we can begin to make sense of some suffering when we understand that God can use it to bring us to Christ or to help us mature in our faith. Yet this still leaves some suffering that we cannot comprehend or account for in any of these ways.

God more than compensates for our suffering

We see in the story of Joseph how God blessed him in the midst of his suffering. Even as a slave to Potiphar, "the LORD was with Joseph so that he prospered . . . the LORD gave him success in everything he did" (Genesis 39:2-3). When he was in prison again "the LORD was with him" (Genesis 39:21) and granted him favor in the eyes of the chief jailer so that he handed over to him the entire prison administration, "because the LORD was with Joseph and gave him success in whatever he did" (Genesis 39:23). God gave him such remarkable supernatural gifts that even Pharaoh recognized him as a man obviously filled with the Spirit of God (Genesis 41:38) and put him in charge of the whole land of Egypt (v. 41). In this position, he had the joy of seeing his entire family reunited and rescued from starvation.

Job, too, went through catastrophic suffering, losing all his wealth, then all his children and finally suffering from the most horrific disease. At the end of the book we read how the Lord blessed the latter part of Job's life more than the first. As well as great wealth, Job had seven sons and three beautiful daughters. He lived to a great age and saw his children, grandchildren and great-grandchildren.

For many, like Joseph and Job, the blessings of God in and through our suffering can match or outweigh the suffering itself. But the New Testament never leads us to assume that this will always be the case. Often we will not experience such blessings in this life.

Rather, every Christian is promised something even greater: the hope of heaven. Paul says, "I consider that our present sufferings are not worth comparing with the glory that will be revealed in us" (Romans 8:18), and on another occasion he wrote, "For our light and momentary troubles are achieving for us an eternal glory that far outweighs them all" (2 Corinthians 4:17).

Gavin Reid, the former Bishop of Maidstone, tells of a boy in his congregation who shattered his back falling down the stairs at the age of one and who had consequently been in and out of hospital. When Gavin interviewed him in church, the boy remarked that "God is fair."

Gavin stopped him and asked, "How old are you?"

The boy replied, "Seventeen."

"How many years have you spent in hospital?"

The boy answered, "Thirteen years."

He was asked, "Do you think that is fair?"

He replied, "God's got all of eternity to make it up to me."

God has indeed got all of eternity to make it up to us, and the New Testament is full of promises about how wonderful heaven will be. All creation will be restored. Jesus will return to earth to establish a new heaven and a new earth (Revelation 21:1). There will be no more crying, for there will be no more pain and suffering. We will change our frail, decaying, mortal bodies for a body like that of Jesus' glorious resurrected body. We shall be reunited with all those who have died "in Christ" and we shall spend eternity together in the presence of the Lord. As Martin Luther once said, "I would not give one moment of heaven for all the joys and riches of the world, even if it lasted for thousands and thousands of years."

We live in a materialistic world that has almost entirely lost its eternal perspective. We need to take a long-term view and understand the suffering of this life in the context of eternity. This is not "pie in the sky when you die." As the theologian Alister McGrath points out, that taunt evades the question: "Is it true?" "If the Christian hope of heaven is an illusion, based upon lies, then it must be abandoned as misleading and deceitful. But if it is true, it must be embraced and allowed to transfigure our entire understanding of the place of suffering in life."[10]

God is involved in our suffering

We must be prepared to acknowledge that there is no simple definitive answer to the "Why?" of suffering. We may approach the problem from a different perspective: God is a God who suffers alongside us.

This fourth insight is perhaps the most important of all. I once heard the late theologian John Stott say, "I could never myself believe in God, if it were not for the cross." God is not a God who is immune to suffering. He is not looking on as an impassive observer far removed from the suffering world. We see that throughout the Bible and, supremely, we see it in the cross. He is, in the words of Tertullian, "the crucified God." God was "in Christ," reconciling the world to himself (2 Corinthians 5:19). He became one of us; He suffered in all the ways in which we suffer. He does not just know about suffering—He has suffered Himself; He knows what we are feeling when we suffer.

In 1967, a beautiful athletic teenager named Joni Eareckson had a terrible diving accident at Chesapeake Bay that left her a quadriplegic. Gradually, after the bitterness, anger, rebellion, and despair, she came to trust the sovereignty of God. She built a new life of painting (using her mouth to hold the paintbrush) and public speaking. One night, three years after the accident, she realized that Jesus empathized with her completely. It had not occurred to her before that on the cross Jesus was in a similar pain to hers, unable to move, also paralysed.[11]

The playlet *The Long Silence* powerfully makes the same point:

At the end of time, billions of people were scattered on a great plain before God's throne.

Most shrank back from the brilliant light before them. But some groups near the front talked heatedly—not with cringing shame, but with belligerence.

"Can God judge us? How can he know about suffering?" snapped a young brunette. She ripped open a sleeve to reveal a tattooed number from a Nazi concentration camp. "We endured terror . . . beatings . . . torture . . . death!"

In another group a young man lowered his collar. "What about this?" he demanded, showing an ugly rope burn. "Lynched . . . for no crime but being black!"

In another crowd, a pregnant schoolgirl with sullen eyes. "Why should I suffer?" she murmured. "It wasn't my fault."

Far out across the plain there were hundreds of such groups. Each had a complaint against God for the evil and suffering he permitted in his world. How lucky God was to live in heaven where all was sweetness and light, where there was no weeping or fear, no hunger or hatred. What did God know of all that man had been forced to endure in this world? For God leads a pretty sheltered life, they said.

So each of these groups sent forth their leader, chosen because he had suffered the most. A Jew, a young black man, a person from Hiroshima, a horribly deformed arthritic, a thalidomide child. In the center of the plain they consulted with each other. At last they were ready to present their case. It was rather clever.

Before God could be qualified to be their judge, he must endure what they had endured. Their decision was that God should be sentenced to live on earth—as a man!

"Let him be born a Jew. Let the legitimacy of his birth be doubted. Give him a work so difficult that even his family will think him out of his mind when he tries to do it. Let him be betrayed by his closest friends. Let him face false charges, be tried by a prejudiced jury and convicted by a cowardly judge. Let him be tortured."

"At the last, let him see what it means to be terribly alone. Then let him die. Let him die so that there can be no doubt that he died. Let there be a great host of witnesses to verify it."

As each leader announced his portion of the sentence, loud murmurs of approval went up from the throng of people assembled.

And when the last had finished pronouncing sentence, there was a long silence. No one uttered another word. No one moved. For suddenly all knew that God had already served his sentence.[12]

Of course, this story is not an analogy: God does not have to serve a sentence, nor does He have to justify Himself. The weakness of the illustration is that it places humanity in judgment over God. As we have already seen, we cannot judge God, because our understanding is too limited. He is too far above and beyond our comprehension. But the story does make the point that God is at the heart of all suffering, alongside us. He was willing to enter into our pain, to become "a man of suffering, and familiar with pain" (Isaiah 53:3). The knowledge of His suffering removes what theologian Jürgen Moltmann has called the "suffering in suffering." It is an extraordinary thing to know that the God of all creation can be with us in our darkest moments. We are not alone in our pain. When we suffer, He suffers with us.

How do we respond to suffering?

When we are suffering we will not always be able to work out why. God never told Job why he was suffering but He told him there was a good reason. He pointed out that Job knew very little about the universe and asked him to trust God. The book of Job is not so much about why God allows suffering as it is about how we should respond to suffering.

The questions we need to ask ourselves are these:

First, "Is this suffering a result of my own sin?" If it is, we can ask God to reveal the specific sin. God will never leave us with a nebulous feeling of guilt. That kind of condemnation may come from Satan, but never from God. If there is a particular sin, we need to repent and ask for God's forgiveness and cleansing.

Second, we need to ask, "What are you saying to me through this?" There may be some particular lesson God wants to teach us.

Third, we need to ask, "What do you want me to do?" Fourth, others in the church can be of great help to us. Good Christian friends can help us discern between true and false guilt, help us to hear from God and be a support and encouragement to us to ensure we do not give up, despite the circumstances. We can "carry each other's burdens" (Galatians 6:2).

Next, we need to hold on to our hope. This life is always a mixture of battle and blessing and, in times of battle, we need to remember that they do not last forever and often blessing is just around the corner. Whether it is or not, we can be sure that one day we will go to be with the Lord forever. Meanwhile, we need to keep our eyes fixed on Him (Hebrews 12:2), knowing that He is more than able to sympathize with us, as He has suffered more than we ever will.

When we see others suffering, we are called to show compassion. In the face of great suffering, attempts to rationalize can be counter-productive. Even if their suffering is caused by their own sin, we are in no position to throw stones. We are all sinners, and we need to be very careful about making judgments. Not all suffering, as we have seen, is directly related to sin. Usually, the most positive thing that we can do is to put an arm around the person and "weep with those who weep" (Romans 12:15, RSV).

We are right to resist suffering because, as we have seen, it is an alien intrusion into God's world. Jesus fought against suffering wherever He came across it. He fed the hungry, healed the sick, and raised the dead. He saw His ministry in terms of preaching good news to the poor, proclaiming freedom to the captives, and recovery of sight to the blind and releasing the oppressed. We are called to follow in His steps.

Finally, and in summary, we need to come back yet again to the cross of Christ. For it is here that we begin to understand why a God of love should allow suffering.

First, we see that human beings abused their God-given freedom when they chose to nail Jesus to the cross. And yet God used that very abuse, enabling Jesus on the cross to pay the price for that sin, and for all sin through all time.

Second, we see God working through suffering. Those who nailed Jesus to the cross intended it for evil, but God intended it for good. The cross is ultimately a victory because it holds the key to salvation.

Third, we see that God more than compensates for suffering. Jesus, who "for the joy set before him endured the cross" (Hebrews 12:2), saw ahead to His resurrection and, as a result of that, to our own resurrection and eternity with Him.

Fourth, and most important of all, we see that God Himself is not removed from suffering. He participated in the suffering of the cross and He suffers for us and with us now. Just as, in Jesus' life, suffering did not mark the end, it is not to have the last word in our lives either. In raising Jesus from the dead to eternal life, God revealed that nothing—no suffering, or even death itself—can separate us from the love of God and eternal life in Him.

CHAPTER 2

WHAT ABOUT OTHER RELIGIONS?

The impression is often given that Christianity is dying out of traditionally Christian Western societies. Two stories are often told.

The first is that other religions are gradually taking over. The second impression, which is becoming increasingly popular, is that the Western world is rapidly becoming secular.

Actually, both these impressions are misleading in part.

For example, only 6 percent of the population of the U.K. are adherents of other faiths. Some 11 percent go to Christian churches and the majority would probably go to a Christian church if they went anywhere.[1]

Worldwide, Christianity is by far the largest "religion." According to the *Encyclopedia Britannica*, it has 2.2 billion adherents worldwide, amounting to around 34 percent of the world population. There are 1.3 billion Muslims, 870 million Hindus and 376 million Buddhists, in addition to many other smaller groupings such as Jews, Sikhs, Bahais and tribal religions.[2] Atheists amount to a mere 2.5 percent of the world population.

Even if Christianity predominates, we still need to face the question of what Christians say about other religions.

One of the results of globalization is that religious identity has taken on more importance in the twenty-first century. Professor David Ford, of Cambridge University, calls our world "complexly both religious and secular." In such a world, questions of what Christians say about other religions soon arise. Modern society and communication have made us all increasingly aware of other faiths. Many of us have significant personal contact with people of other faiths—in the classroom, neighborhood, work and social activities. We are also brought into regular contact with other faiths through TV, films, the internet and radio. What are we to say about these other religions?

Is Jesus the only way to God?

The answer of the New Testament is an emphatic "Yes."

Jesus Himself said, "I am the way and the truth and the life. No one comes to the Father except through me" (John 14:6). He claimed to be the way to God and, indeed, the only way. The late columnist Bernard Levin made the point that Jesus used unequivocal language:

> I take it that a religion which claims to be following the truth, the whole truth and nothing but the truth must, even if only by a process of elimination, think that the other religions are, for all their holiness and worship, mistaken. I, of all people, should not bandy scripture with experts, but in these ecumenical days it is surely reasonable to ask Christianity what its founder meant when he said, "None shall come to the Father but by me." I do not offer those words to give offence, but many a devout Christian is worried by them, and many a bishop, opening his heart to other faiths, must be hard put to it to provide an answer. I doubt if you will get a very convincing answer anywhere, bishop or no bishop.[3]

In Acts 4, when Peter and John healed the crippled man outside the Temple, a large crowd gathered. Peter proclaimed Jesus as the "author of life" who had been crucified but was now resurrected and glorified. They were arrested and put on trial and asked "by what power" the crippled man had been healed. Peter, "filled with the Holy Spirit," replied that it was "by the name of Jesus Christ of Nazareth" and that "salvation is found in no one else, for there is no other name under heaven given to mankind by which we must be saved" (Acts 4:12).

Peter, inspired by the Holy Spirit, is unequivocal. Jesus is the only name that can save. His answer is consistent with the rest of the New Testament. St. Paul is equally emphatic: "For there is one God and one mediator between God and mankind, Christ Jesus, the man" (1 Timothy 2:5). So the writer of Hebrews warns us that there is no other means of escape except through Jesus Christ: "How shall we escape if we ignore so great a salvation?" (Hebrews 2:3).

In what way is Jesus to be considered the only way to God? Christians believe that Jesus brings salvation. Jesus comes to bridge the gap between humanity and God that first opened up in the fall, and which exists wherever God's people turn away from Him in self-centredness and sin, failing to recognize and worship God as the giver of all the good gifts that surround us.

Jesus is uniquely able to bridge that gap of sin, first, because of *who* He is. Peter proclaimed Him as the "Holy and Righteous One" (Acts 3:14), the "author of life" (v. 15). He is the one the prophets foretold (v. 18). He is the "Christ" (v. 20). He is the one whom the early church worshipped as God. This sets Him apart from the leaders of the other great world religions. Muslims do not like being described as Muhammadans, because they do not worship Muhammad. "No one in the Islamic world has ever dreamed of according to him divine honors—he would have been the first to reject any such suggestion as blasphemy."[4] It is not clear whether Buddha believed in the existence of God as such, but it is clear that he did not consider himself to be a god.[5]

Second, Jesus is unique in His achievement, or what He has *done*. As we have seen previously, Peter asserts, "salvation is found in no one else, for there is no other name under heaven given to mankind by which we must be saved" (Acts 4:12). We all need a savior because we have all sinned and we cannot save ourselves from the results of sin. None of the other great religions even claims to have a savior. "The English Buddhist, Maurice Walsh, pointed out that the Buddhist view of Buddha is very different from the Christian view of Christ. He stressed that the Buddha is thought of as a Teacher—not as a Savior."[6] Likewise, Muhammad is regarded as a prophet—not as a savior. In Islam, sinners will face judgment without forgiveness—the obedience and righteousness of their lives will be weighed against their sin.

By contrast, Jesus is the one who brings salvation. He saves us from our guilt, He saves us from the addictive power of sin and He saves us from the judgment we all deserve.

Third, Jesus is unique in comparison with the leaders of the other great faiths of the world in His *resurrection*. Peter described Him as the one "whom God raised from the dead" (Acts 4:10). The resurrection is a unique event in the history of the world.

The Pali Canon of Buddhism records the great entrance of . . . the Buddha into Nirvana . . . but there is no suggestion that the Buddha will continue to be present with his followers after his death; the *dhamma*, the teaching, will take his place and will be their guide . . . the exact date of the death of the prophet Muhammad is known. No one has ever supposed that he survived physical death.[7]

By contrast, the resurrection of Jesus lies at the heart of the Christian faith. Jesus Christ is alive today. We can know Him, and it is only because of this living relationship that the gap between God and humanity, which the Bible describes, is bridged. For Christians, Jesus, the unique Son of God, the unique Savior, the one uniquely raised from the dead, is the only way to God.

If Jesus is the only way to God, this immediately raises two further questions: first, "What do we say about other religions?" Second, "What about those who have never heard about Jesus?"

What do we say about other religions?

The fact that Jesus is the only way to God does not mean that we simply write off all other religions as completely wrong, misguided or demonic. Jesus said, "I am the truth." In Him, ultimate truth is to be found and He is the standard by which all truth claims are to be tested. But this does not mean that parts of the truth cannot be found in other religions. Indeed, we would expect to find truth in other religions for at least three reasons.

First, although God's revelation of Himself in Jesus, witnessed to in Scripture, is unique and final, God has partially revealed Himself in creation. "The heavens declare the glory of God; the skies proclaim the work of his hands" (Psalm 19:1). The pinnacle of His creation is human life. As Sir Isaac Newton, the brilliant physicist and mathematician, said, "In the absence of any other proof, the thumb alone would convince me of God's existence."

Therefore, the psalmist says, only a fool can claim that "there is no God" (Psalm 14:1; 53:1). "For since the creation of the world God's invisible qualities—his eternal power and divine nature—have been clearly seen, being understood from what has been made, so that people are without excuse" (Romans 1:20). From creation, it is possible for men and women to find out the truth about God's existence and gain an insight into His character: His power and His glory. The evidence provided by creation is available to all, and could therefore be grasped by other religions. It is this God to whom the great monotheistic faiths reach.

Second, human beings are made in the image of God and God has given us a conscience with which to distinguish right and wrong. As Paul put it, "Indeed, when Gentiles, who do not have the law, do by nature things required by the law . . . they show that the requirements of the law are written on their hearts, their consciences also bearing witness, and their thoughts now accusing them and at other times even defending them" (Romans 2:14-15). Thus, it is not surprising that the essence of "the golden rule" ("Do to others what you would have them do to you"—Matthew 7:12) is contained in almost every religion from Confucius (551-479 BC) onwards.

Third, in every heart there is a hunger for God. God has "set eternity in the human heart" (Ecclesiastes 3:11). Deep down no one is satisfied by materialism; we know there is more to life. There is a God-shaped gap in the heart of every human being. This hunger drives us to search for God. It is one of the explanations as to why there are so few atheists in the world and why so many seek earnestly after God.

It is understandable then that we find good in many religions. Of course, we will be challenged as Christians by aspects of the lives of adherents to other religions, for example, their commitment, their devotion or their dedication to what they believe.

It also explains why there is often a certain continuity for those who become Christians from other faiths. Bishop Lesslie Newbigin, who was a bishop in South India for forty years, spoke of:

> . . . an element of continuity which is confirmed in the experience of many who have become converts to Christianity from other religions. Even though this conversion involves a radical discontinuity, yet there is often the strong conviction afterwards that it was the living and true God who was dealing with them in the days of their pre-Christian wrestlings.[8]

This conviction goes at least as far back as St. Augustine, whose *Confessions* describe the way in which the Holy Spirit was leading him years before his conversion to Christ.

Nevertheless, it is illogical to assert that all religions are equally true or that all religions lead to God. The theologian Alister McGrath points out that some world religions are avowedly non-theistic and that "a religion can hardly lead to God if it explicitly denies the existence of a god or any gods."[9] Equally, it is absurd to suggest that a religion that asserts that there is a god and one which asserts there is no god are both equally true. Since there are contradictions between the religions, there must be error somewhere. Indeed, we would expect to find error in other religions.

We are all fallen human beings (Christian and non-Christian alike), and none of us can find God by ourselves. But God has revealed Himself in the person of Jesus who is "the truth." Only in Jesus Christ do we find infallible truth. That is not to say that Christians are infallible, or that our understanding of the truth is infallible, but that God's revelation in Jesus Christ is infallible. He is the standard by which all truth claims must be examined.

By putting other religions alongside God's revelation in Jesus Christ, we see that they contain both truth and error. There may be dark aspects to other religions and, at times, the Bible is very strong in its opposition to the practices of some other religions (e.g. 1 Corinthians 10:21). Of course, there may also be a dark side to the way some people use Christianity to certain ends, but there is no dark side to God's revelation in Jesus Christ.

Some would suggest that this is an arrogant, narrow-minded, illiberal and unhelpful belief in today's world. And yet, C. S. Lewis reminds us, quite the opposite is true:

> If you are a Christian you do not have to believe that all the other religions
> are simply wrong all through. If you are an atheist you do have to believe
> that the main point in all the religions of the whole world is simply one huge
> mistake. If you are a Christian, you are free to think that all those religions,
> even the queerest ones, contain at least some hint of the truth. When I was
> an atheist I had to try to persuade myself that most of the human race have
> always been wrong about the question that mattered to them most; when
> I became a Christian I was able to take a more liberal view. But, of course,

being a Christian does mean thinking that where Christianity differs from other religions, Christianity is right and they are wrong. As in arithmetic— there is only one right answer to a sum, and all other answers are wrong; but some of the wrong answers are much nearer being right than others.[10]

What about those who have never heard about Jesus?

This is the second question raised by the New Testament's claim that there is no other way to God. If we can be saved only through Jesus, are all the rest damned? If so, is that not unjust? In exploring this "searching issue," five points emerge.

First, the Bible is a practical book, not a philosophical one. It does not answer hypothetical questions directly. Appreciating this dimension of what the Bible is will help us in exploring many "searching issues," not just this one. Indeed, this question can only ever be hypothetical, since it can be asked only by someone who has heard about Jesus.

Second, we can be sure that God will be just. When Abraham asked the rhetorical question, "Will not the Judge of all the earth do right?" (Genesis 18:25), he clearly expected the answer, "Yes, of course he will." We need not fear that God will be unjust. He will be more just than we are, not less. On judgment day, every right-thinking person will say of God's judgment: "That is completely just."

Third, what we do know is that no one will be saved by their religious behavior. We are saved by God's undeserved love through faith in Jesus Christ (Ephesians 2:8). He died for us so that we can be forgiven. We receive salvation when we accept the gift by faith.

Fourth, it is important to note that it is at least possible to be saved by grace, through faith, even if someone has never heard of Jesus. "Abraham believed God, and it was credited to him as righteousness" (Romans 4:3). Paul tells us that David also speaks of "the blessedness of the one to whom God credits righteousness apart from works" (Romans 4:6). This is possible because the cross is effective for all those who lived before as well as after Jesus. Abraham and David were forgiven because of what Jesus was to do for them on the cross. They did not have the advantage that we have of knowing how it is possible to be forgiven. They did not have the assurance that we have as a result of knowing about "Jesus Christ and him crucified"

(1 Corinthians 2:2). Nevertheless, Paul tells us that they were justified by faith.

In the same way, the person who lived at the time of Jesus or after Him would be justified by faith—even if they had not heard about Him. So Jesus tells us in the parable of the Pharisee and the tax collector that the tax collector who said, "God, have mercy on me, a sinner," went home justified before God (Luke 18:9–14). Surely the same is true for anyone today who has not heard of Jesus but did what the tax collector did.

> So the essential elements would seem to be a God-given sense of sin or need, and a self-abandonment to God's mercy. If a man of whom this is true subsequently hears and understands the gospel, then I myself believe that he would be among the company of those, whom one does sometimes meet on the mission field, who welcome and accept it at once, saying (in effect): "This is what I have been waiting for all these years. Why didn't you come and tell me before?" And if he never hears the gospel here on earth, then I suppose that he will wake up, as it were, on the other side of the grave to worship the One in whom, without understanding it at the time, he had found the mercy of God."[11]

Fifth, as John Stott points out, there are biblical grounds for great optimism. Abraham's descendants (spiritual as well as physical) will be "as numerous as the stars in the sky and as the sand on the seashore" (Genesis 22:17). In the same vein we seem to be assured by Paul that many more people will be saved than lost because Christ's work in causing salvation will be more successful than Adam's in causing ruin and because God's grace in bringing life will overflow 'much more' than Adam's trespass in bringing death."[12] (See Romans 5:2.)

If that is the case, why should we bother to tell others about Jesus? First, because the route we have taken all the way through this chapter has begun with Jesus and set out into the world: who He is, what He has done, the reality that He is risen. We are compelled to proclaim the glory of Jesus Christ. Second, because Jesus commanded us to go into all the world and tell the good news. Third, because without knowing about Jesus no one could have the assurance of forgiveness and the abundant life He offers both in this life and in the life to come. For Jesus is not only the way and the truth, He is also "the life."

What should we do?

We have no excuse. No one who has read this chapter will ever be able to say, "I never heard about Jesus." So also we have no other escape. As the writer of Hebrews warns us all, "How shall we escape if we ignore" (Hebrews 2:3).

As far as others are concerned, our task is to tell them the good news about Jesus. If the early Christians had not been willing to tell the good news about Jesus to those who already had a religion of their own, Christianity would have died in a generation.

> The Christian points to the one Lord Jesus Christ as the Lord of all men . . . the Church does not apologise for the fact that it wants all men to know Jesus Christ and to follow him. Its very calling is to proclaim the Gospel to the ends of the earth. It cannot make any restrictions in this respect. Whether people have a high, a low or a primitive religion, whether they have sublime ideals or a defective morality makes no fundamental difference in this respect. All must hear the Gospel.[13]

Of course we need to be humble and sensitive. Christians are no better than those of other religions or those of no religion. We are all in the same boat: we all need a savior and there is no room for arrogance.

Second, we need to be positive. In Acts 4, Peter did not attack other faiths. He preached the good news about Jesus.

Third, we need to be respectful. We need to respect everyone as being made in the image of God—whether they are Christians or not.

Finally, we need to be courageous. The early Christians were unashamed witnesses to Jesus. Their message was unpopular and it got them into trouble. But they did not stop. We need to do the same in an age when tolerance, not truth, is the order of the day.

As we noted at the beginning, we live today in a world where there is a plurality of ideas, both religious and secular, vying together in the marketplace of truth. Yet, it is important to remember that "the pluralism of the first and second centuries AD was the greatest in extent and intensity the world has ever seen." The world as Jesus knew it when He walked the earth was also complex in its religion and ideas. As Michael Green goes on to say, "Far from closing our options, pluralism allows us to proclaim an undiluted gospel in the public square and in the supermarket of faiths, allowing others the same right. Let the truth prevail and let craven silence be banished."[14]

CHAPTER 3

IS THERE A CONFLICT BETWEEN SCIENCE AND CHRISTIANITY?

The image often portrayed by the media, for whom any confrontation is news, is that Christian belief and science are in direct conflict. An article entitled "God vs. Science" in *Time* magazine wrote about how some contemporary critics of religion are:

> Radicalized enough to publicly pick an ancient scab: the idea that science and religion, far from being complementary responses to the unknown, are at utter odds—or, as Yale psychologist Paul Bloom has written bluntly, "Religion and science will always clash." The market seems flooded with books by scientists describing a caged death match between science and God—with science winning, or at least chipping away at faith's underlying verities.[1]

Do "religion and science always clash?" That is the question that this chapter seeks to explore.

First, there have certainly been periods in the history of Christianity when the church has opposed the results of scientific study. Galileo, the seventeenth-century Italian astronomer, found himself in conflict with the Roman Catholic Church over his discovery that planets revolve round the sun. He was tried by the inquisition in Rome, ordered to recant and spent the final eight years of his life under house arrest.

Persecution of scientists did not end in the seventeenth century. As late as 1925, John T. Scopes, a high-school teacher from Drayton, Tennessee, was prosecuted for violating the state law by teaching the theory of evolution. He was convicted and fined $100. On appeal, he was acquitted on the technicality that he had been fined excessively.

Second, it is thought by many that modern scientific study explains everything that was once explained by belief in God, so that such belief is now redundant. Further, it is argued that the assured results of modern science are in direct conflict with the teaching of the Bible. Some would say, for example, that modern science shows that miracles do not happen, whereas the Bible is full of miracles. Others claim that the scientific theory of the gradual evolution of humans and their organisms by natural processes is inconsistent with the account of creation in Genesis 1. The English biologist and agnostic philosopher T. H. Huxley (1825–95), for example, said, "The doctrine of Evolution, if consistently accepted, makes it impossible to believe the Bible." Oxford scientist Richard Dawkins comes to a similar conclusion in a chapter on Darwinism, in which he concludes that "God almost certainly does not exist."[2]

In this chapter I want to look at how science and Christian belief relate to each other and, in particular, whether there is a conflict between "the assured results of modern science" and the Christian faith.

Science and Christian faith are not incompatible

It was the Judeo-Christian worldview that provided the right environment for modern science to emerge. First, the Christian faith is monotheistic. Belief in one God led people to expect a uniformity in nature, with the underlying laws of nature remaining the same in time and space. A universe that was capricious and irregular would not be capable of systematic study.

Second, the Christian doctrine of creation by a rational God of order led scientists to expect a world that was both ordered and intelligible. Sixteenth-century scientists reasoned that the universe must be orderly and worthy of investigation because it was the work of an intelligent creator. "Men became scientific because they expected Law in Nature, and they expected Law in Nature because they believed in a Legislator."[3]

Third, the Christian belief in a transcendent God, separate from nature, meant that experimentation was justified. This would not have been the case under belief systems that regarded forms of matter as gods. Nor would it have been wise to experiment if you believed, as some did, that matter was essentially evil. The Christian worldview was that matter was good, but was not God. So the Christian doctrine of creation "provided an essential matrix for the coming into being of the scientific enterprise."[4]

That Christian belief provided fertile soil for scientific experimentation is recognized by scientists, historians and philosophers. The British Oxford University physicist Dr Peter Hodgson writes, "Christianity provided just those beliefs that are essential for science, and the whole moral climate that encouraged its growth."[5] The historian Herbert Butterfield stated that "science is a child of Christian thought." The philosopher John MacMurray put it like this: "Science is the legitimate child of a great religious movement, and its genealogy goes back to Jesus."[6]

Some of the greatest scientists have been Christians

It is a well-established fact that for much of history Christianity and scientific study have been allies and not opponents.

Nicolaus Copernicus (1473-1543) laid the foundations of modern astronomy and the scientific revolution by suggesting, on mathematical grounds, that the earth traveled round the sun. He held office in the Polish Church as a Canon of Frauenburg Cathedral and described God as "the Best and Most Orderly Workman of all."

Mathematician, physicist and astronomer Galileo Galilei (1564-1642) was the founder of modern mechanics and experimental physics. He argued that the earth was not the center of the universe. Although he was persecuted by the church, he was a devout Roman Catholic Christian and once said, "There are two big books, the book of nature and the book of supernature, the Bible."

The founder of modern optics was the brilliant early astronomer and mathematician Johannes Kepler (1571–1630), best known for his discovery of the three principles of planetary motion. He was a deeply sincere Lutheran and said that he was "thinking God's thoughts after Him."

Perhaps the greatest scientist of all time was Sir Isaac Newton (1642–1727). He was certainly one of the most towering scientific intellects in history. He is well known for his formulation for the laws of gravity. He was also an expert in the field of optics, astronomy, differential calculus and responsible for the first correct analysis of white light. He believed in the inspiration of Scripture and wrote theological as well as scientific books, regarding his theological books as more important. He believed that no sciences were better attested than the religion of the Bible.

Michael Faraday (1791–1867) was one of the greatest scientists of the nineteenth century. He discovered the phenomenon of electromagnetic induction. He was the first to produce an electric current from a magnetic field. He invented the first electric motor and dynamo. Again, the Christian faith was the single most important influence upon him.

The same is true of many other pioneering scientists. Robert Lister pioneered antiseptic surgery; Louis Pasteur originated pasteurization; Gregor Mendel helped form the basis for the science of genetics; Lord Kelvin was a leading light in the foundation of modern physics; James Clerk Maxwell formulated electromagnetic theory. All these leading scientists were Christians.

Professor James Simpson, who paved the way for painless surgery through anesthetics, was asked, "What do you think is the most important discovery of your life?" He replied, "The most important discovery I ever made was when I discovered Jesus Christ."

In our own day there are a large number of scientists who are professing Christians. Christians in Science has over 1,000 members and its US counterpart has over 7,000 members. It would seem that numbers are not declining: "In 1916, researchers asked biologists, physicists, and mathematicians whether they believed in a God who actively communicates with humankind and to whom one may pray in expectation of receiving an answer. About 40 percent answered in the affirmative." Nearly 100 years later, in 1997, the same survey found that the percentage was almost identical. According to a 2009 study by the Pew Research Center, just over 50 percent of American scientists believe in a God, while 40 percent do not.[7]

One of the leading scientists of our generation is Rev. Dr. John Polkinghorne KBE FRS, former Professor of Mathematical Physics and Dean and Chaplain of Trinity Hall, as well as former President of Queen's College, Cambridge. In 2002 he was awarded the prestigious Templeton Prize. He wrote:

> Men of religion can learn from science what the physical world is really like in its structure and long-evolving history. This constrains what religion can say where it speaks of that world as God's creation. He is clearly a patient God who works through process and not by magic. Men of science can receive from religion a deeper understanding than could be obtained from science alone. The physical world's deep mathematical intelligibility (signs of the Mind behind it) and finely tuned fruitfulness (expressive of divine purpose) are reflections of the fact that it is a creation.[8]

We could also note prominent contemporary figures such as Sir John Houghton FRS CBE, a leading UK scientist who was co-chair of the working group of the Intergovernmental Panel on Climate Change (IPCC) for fourteen years. In 2007, Houghton shared the Nobel Peace Prize with former US Vice President Al Gore. He was also Professor in Atmospheric Physics at the University of Oxford, former Chief Executive at the Met Office and he is a founder member of the International Society for Science and Religion.

Another example is Francis Collins, whose conversion to Christianity is described in Chapter 7. As head of the Human Genome Project, he led a team of over 2,000 scientists who collaborated to determine the three billion letters of the human genome—our own DNA instruction book. It would take thirty-one years to read those letters aloud. This information is inside every single one of the one hundred trillion cells in our bodies. Each genome contains enough information to fill a library of about 5,000 books. If all the chromosomes in a single body were laid out end-to-end, they would stretch one hundred billion miles. Our brains alone have a billion nerve cells. As the steward of the study of this great mystery, Collins speaks of "a richly satisfying harmony between the scientific and the spiritual worldviews." He also said, "I am a scientist and a believer, and I find no conflict between those world views."[9]

Science and Scripture do not contradict each other

It is probably true that there are more disagreements and apparent contradictions within science itself than between science and the Christian faith. Nevertheless, it is commonly thought that there are conflicts between science and theology.

One of the alleged conflicts is in the area of miracles.[10] Spinoza (1632–77), the Dutch-Jewish philosopher and the foremost exponent of seventeenth-century rationalism, declared that nothing can "contravene nature's universal laws." He believed in a mechanistic uniformity of nature. The philosopher David Hume defined a miracle as "a violation of the laws of nature."[11] Consequently, he rejected miracles, suggesting they are impossible. However, this is a circular argument. If the laws of nature are defined as completely uniform, then the supernatural is ruled out from the start and it is therefore impossible to believe in miracles, however strong the evidence.

Yet many have pointed to this conflict between the Bible and science. In 1937, the distinguished German physicist Max Planck said, "Faith in miracles must yield ground, step-by-step, before the steady and firm advance of the forces of science, and its total defeat is indubitably a mere matter of time."[12] Planck implied that science now explains what was once thought to be miraculous, which suggests that those who believed in miracles in the past did so because they didn't sufficiently understand the laws of nature. This is not the case. In Jesus' day everyone knew, just as well as we do, that, for example, it is not "natural" for a virgin to have a baby or for someone to rise from the dead. If they had had no knowledge of the laws of nature, then they would not have recognized a miracle in any shape or form. As the famed novelist and English professor C. S. Lewis said, "Belief in miracles, far from depending on an ignorance of the laws of nature, is only possible insofar as those laws are known."[13]

The real issue is, "Is there a God?" If there is, then miracles become a real possibility. If God is God, then He created matter, reason, time, space and all scientific laws, and therefore is at liberty to interfere. If there is no God, then miracles are a problem. But philosophy and science alone will not answer the crucial question. Scientific laws are not laws like the laws of pure mathematics, which cannot be broken. Rather, they are descriptive. As John Stott put it, "I am not suggesting that miracles are an adequate basis for theism. But, once we have come on other grounds to believe in God . . . it becomes logical to affirm, and illogical to deny, the possibility of the miraculous. For 'natural laws' describe God's activity; they do not control it."[14]

Is there a conflict between creation and evolution?

The second area of alleged conflict is the theory of evolution and the biblical account of creation. Is there an irreconcilable conflict?

The first point to note is that much of the theory of evolution is still only theory. It is necessary to distinguish between micro- and macro-evolution. Micro-evolution (which could not conceivably be said to conflict with the Bible) means the variation and development within a species. The horse, for example, has increased greatly in size and developed in other ways over time. This kind of evolution has been observed and there is overwhelming evidence for it.

Macro-evolution, on the other hand, means evolution from one species to another—the most famous example being from apes to humans. It is often thought of as fact but is still unproved and remains a theory that is not accepted by all scientists.[15] It is important to stress the provisionality of all scientific theories. The most striking example in modern times is Newtonian physics, which was treated with the utmost respect and regarded as virtually incontestable until Einstein and others showed that its laws broke down for the very, very small (where Quantum Mechanics becomes relevant) and the very, very fast (where Relativity becomes relevant). Particular versions of theories of evolution are still taught in schools as if they are the aforementioned "assured results of modern science." To regard a scientific theory as more than provisional is bad science.

The second important point is that there are many different interpretations of Genesis held by sincere Christians. Some believe in a literal six-day creation. The Creation Research Society, formed in 1963 as a committee of ten scientists in Michigan, USA, whose membership is limited to scientists having at least a graduate degree in a natural or applied science, now has hundreds of members. They believe that all types of living things were made by direct acts of God during the creation week. Whatever biological changes have occurred since then have been only within the original created kinds.

Other Christians interpret Genesis 1 differently. They point out that the Hebrew word for "day" (*yom*) has many different meanings, even within Scripture. Since the sun did not appear until day four, the writer probably did not mean twenty-four-hour days. The word *yom* can mean a long period of time. When read in this way, it is not in conflict with the prevailing scientific view of the vast age of the universe, nor is it in conflict with a gradual evolution in which God not only started the process, but worked within it to produce a system that culminated in human life. They point out that the chronological order of Genesis 1 begins with plants, then animals, and finally humans, in perhaps a similar way to that now accepted by evolutionary theorists.

Some add the suggestion that Genesis is about information fed in at intervals ("And God said . . ."). The feeding in of information takes place in a short period of time. The working out of that information takes much longer. They point out that this corresponds remarkably with the theory of the Big Bang, where the essential things happened within the first few minutes.

Many Christians read Genesis 1 as poetic in form, which is not necessarily connected with chronological events in history. It is a pre-scientific and non-scientific account of creation, dealing with matters outside the scope of science. Poetic language can be true without being literally true. When the psalmist wrote, ". . . the world is established, firm and secure." (Psalm 93:1), he was using a poetic image. But Galileo's opponents took it literally and argued that the earth was stationary and that theories of the earth orbiting the sun were wrong. These Christians feel that, in the same way, the early chapters of Genesis should not be taken literally. They say that there is strong evidence for macro-evolutionary theory and that it is now accepted by the vast majority of scientists who argue that the fossil evidence is inconsistent with a literal interpretation of the Genesis account. Those who take this view argue that what matters is that it is God who created and sustains the laws of physics and nature that evolved over time, culminating in human life.

Whichever view one takes, it is clear that there is not necessarily a conflict between science and Scripture. In the light of the uncertainty and the difference of opinions among genuine Christians, I think it is unwise to be too dogmatic about the issue (certainly if, like me, you are neither a scientist nor a theologian).

The main point of Genesis 1 is not to answer the questions "How?" and "When?" (the scientific questions), but the questions "Why?" and "Who?"(the theological questions). The Bible is not primarily a scientific book, but a theological one. It offers a personal explanation more than a scientific one. The scientific explanation does not prove or disprove the personal one. Rather it is complementary. Even Stephen Hawking, arguably the most brilliant scientist of his generation, has admitted that "science may solve the problem of how the universe began, but it cannot answer the question: why does the universe bother to exist?"[16]

Dr. John Lennox uses the following illustration:

Suppose I wheel in the most magnificent cake ever seen and I had in front of me various fellows of every academic and learned society in the world and I picked the top men and I tell them to analyse the cake for me. So out steps the world famous nutritionist and he talks about the balance of the various foods that form this cake. Then a leading biochemist analyses the cake at the bio-chemical level. Then a chemist says, "Well, yes, of course, but now we must get down to the very basic chemicals that form this." Then the physicist comes on and says, "Well, yes, these people have told you something, but you really need to get down to the electrons and the protons and the quarks." And last of all the stage is occupied by the mathematician. And he says, "Ultimately you need to understand the fundamental equations governing the motion of all the electrons and protons in this cake." And they finish and it is a magnificent analysis of the cake. And then I turn round to them and I say, "Ladies and Gentlemen, I've just got one more question for you. Tell me *why* the cake was made." And there in front of them stands Aunt Mathilda who made the cake. It's only when the person who made the cake is prepared to disclose why she's made it that they'll ever understand *why*. No amount of scientific analysis, however exhaustive and detailed, can answer that question. And then Aunt Mathilda in the end says, "I'll let you out of your misery. I've made the cake for my nephew Johnny—it's his birthday next week."

Dr. John Lennox affirms that "No amount of scientific analysis of this planet on which we stand will tell you why it was made unless the Creator chooses Himself to speak. The fantastic thing is that He has spoken and what He has spoken is called Genesis." There is therefore no necessary conflict between evolution, which attempts to describe the mechanism of creation, and Genesis, which describes the meaning of creation.

Science and Scripture complement each other

God has revealed Himself both in creation and supremely in Jesus Christ, as witnessed to in the Scriptures. Science is the study of God's general revelation in creation. Biblical theology is the study of God's "special"revelation in Jesus and the Scriptures.

The psalmist speaks of this general revelation in the natural world:

The heavens declare the glory of God; the skies proclaim the work of his hands. Day after day they pour forth speech; night after night they reveal knowledge. They have no speech, they use no words; no sound is heard from them. Yet their voice goes out into all the earth, their words to the ends of the world.

Psalm 19:1-4a

The apostle Paul makes a similar claim: "For since the creation of the world God's invisible qualities—his eternal power and divine nature—have been clearly seen, being understood from what has been made, so that people are without excuse" (Romans 1:20; see also Acts 14:17; 17:22-28).

Some have argued, as William Paley did in the eighteenth century, that the existence of God could be proved from "natural theology," i.e., God's general revelation in creation. Perhaps that is going too far. What can be said is that God the Creator has made a world in which there is much to suggest the presence of "more than meets the eye," and He has not left it wholly without marks of His character.

There are two main arguments for this. First, there is the argument that since everything has a cause there must be a first cause. The popular version of this is in the story of the Hyde Park orator in London who was attacking belief in God. He argued that the world just happened. As he spoke, a soft tomato was thrown at him. "Who threw that?" he demanded angrily. A voice from the back of the crowd replied, "No one threw it—it threw itself."

This argument is not a proof, but it is a pointer. It is easier to believe that God created something out of nothing than to believe that nothing created something out of nothing. Towards the end of his life, Charles Darwin wrote of

> the impossibility of conceiving this immense and wonderful universe including man as a result of blind chance or necessity. When thus reflecting, I feel compelled to look to a first cause having an intelligent mind in some degree analogous to that of man and I deserve to be called a theist.[17]

The second argument is based on the evidence of design. Again, this does not amount to a "proof," but is a powerful indicator.

Professor Chandra Wickramasinghe, who comes from a Buddhist background, has said, "The chances that life just occurred on earth are about as unlikely as a typhoon blowing through a junkyard and constructing a Boeing 747."

The matter of design has recently come to the fore with the "anthropic principle." The physical constraints of nature are so finely tuned that, if they were slightly different, we would not exist.

> In the early expansion of the universe there has to be a close balance between the expansive energy (driving things apart) and the force of gravity (pulling things together). If expansion dominated then matter would fly apart too rapidly for condensation into galaxies and stars to take place. Nothing interesting could happen in so thinly spread a world. On the other hand, if gravity dominated the world would collapse in on itself again before there was time for the processes of life to get going. For us to be possible requires a balance between the effects of expansion and contraction which at a very early epoch in the universe's history (the Planck time) has to differ from equality by not more than 1 in 1060. The numerate will marvel at such

a degree of accuracy. For the non-numerate I will borrow an illustration from Paul Davies[18] of what that accuracy means. He points out that it is the same as aiming at a target an inch wide on the other side of the observable universe, twenty thousand million light years away, and hitting the mark![19]

Stephen Hawking makes the point that,

> If the density of the universe one second after the Big Bang had been greater by one part in a thousand billion, the universe would have recollapsed after ten years. On the other hand, if the density of the universe at that time had been less by the same amount, the universe would have been essentially empty since it was about ten years old. How was it that the initial density of the universe was chosen so carefully? Maybe there is some reason why the universe should have precisely the critical density?[20]

Although he does not believe in a creator God, his own theory would seem to point in that direction.

Nor is it just life that has to be explained. It is intelligent life, the human mind, the rational structure of the world, beauty, human love, friendship, and justice. These are all dimensions of reality that point beyond chemical and biological laws. Could all this simply be the result of blind chance and natural selection, with no intelligent mind behind the process?

The evidence of science may point to the existence of God. General revelation suggests the tremendous power, intelligence, and imagination of a personal creator. But without the special revelation of Jesus Christ as witnessed to in the Scriptures, we would have known little about Him.

Albert Einstein, writing from a Jewish perspective, said, "A legitimate conflict between science and religion cannot exist. Science without religion is lame; religion without science is blind." Science without religion is lame for a number of reasons. First, we cannot find the God of the Bible through science alone. "Unfortunately for the scientifically minded, God is not discoverable or demonstrable by purely scientific means. But that really proves nothing; it simply means that the wrong instruments are being used for the job."[21] We need God's special revelation as well as His general revelation. The first six verses of Psalm 19 speak of God's general revelation.

The next verses speak of God's special revelation through His law. It is only through His special revelation that we can find "the God and Father of our Lord Jesus Christ."

Second, science cannot speak to the deepest needs of men and women. Lewis Wolpert writing in *The Times* said, "Scientists, or anyone else, without religion, have to face a world in which there is no real purpose, no meaning to torment and joy, and accept that when we are dead we vanish, that there is no after-life."[22] Science has nothing to say to these deep levels of human experience. It cannot deal with the problem of loneliness or hearts broken by grief. Science is unable to solve the moral dilemmas of humankind. It has no remedy for the problem of unforgiven sin and guilt. Only in the cross of Christ do we find the answer to these problems.

Bestselling novelist Susan Howatch had houses in several countries and drove a Porsche and a Mercedes. She said that, after the break-up of her marriage, "God seized me by the scruff of the neck" and she became a Christian. Recently, she gave £1 million to Cambridge University to finance a lectureship in theology and natural science, having come to the conclusion that science and theology were "two aspects of the truth." We need science and scientists. Our civilization owes a great deal to their work. But more than that we need Christianity and we need Jesus Christ.

CHAPTER 4

WHAT ABOUT THE NEW SPIRITUALITY?

A quick trip to the "Mind, Body, Spirit" shelf of most bookshops or to the "Religion and Spirituality" section of online retailers reveals a bewildering range of contemporary answers to questions about who we are, about how we can change and live more meaningful lives, and about God or the divine.

Some approach these questions in an eclectic way, pulling together words of wisdom and the sentiments of respected thinkers from a variety of religious traditions (or none) down through the ages, offering people whichever perspectives and answers best resonate with their lives.

Others invite people to commit themselves to a particular path, whether that of the "New Age," of a particular pop psychology or form of self-help, or of ideas taken from Buddhism and eastern spiritualities. Some of these ideas are quite new, while others are older ideas and movements that are regaining popularity. Together they make up what we might group under the broad heading "the new spirituality."

Statistics suggest that more than 92 million books were sold in the "Mind, Body, Spirit" category in the US in 1999, around 9 percent of total book sales. Of those, 34 percent were inspirational titles, 28 percent diet related, 16 percent psychology, and 13 percent New Age. Rhonda Byrne's *The Secret*, a manifesto for "positive thinking" published in 2006, remained at the top of *The New York Times* Best Seller list for 146 consecutive weeks. Eckhart Tolle's recent book *The Power of Now: A Guide to Spiritual Enlightenment* spent 1,986 days in Amazon's Top 100.

All this provides yet another indicator that people everywhere are thinking about ways in which there might be *more* to life. In a 2005 Europe-wide survey, 74 percent of people answered that they think about the meaning of life either "sometimes" or "often," while over two-thirds of the group who said "yes" to that question also answered that they believe not in a "conventional" God but rather in some sort of spirit or life force.[1] Meanwhile, in the United States, the number of people who identified themselves as "pagan" more than doubled between 2001 and 2008, while those identifying themselves as "spiritualist" shot up from 116,000 to 420,000.[2]

My perspective as a Christian living in the Western world is that we live in extraordinary and changing times. We are living in the midst of a revolution in the way we think and the way in which we look at the world. At the same time as a scientific worldview is beginning to enter popular consciousness more deeply, the restrictiveness of what we could call the Enlightenment worldview and framework is also being questioned by many.

In pre-Enlightenment times, reason was viewed as a tool of understanding but was subordinated to the revealed truth of Christianity, which was seen as thoroughly supernatural. The seventeenth and eighteenth centuries saw a shift in the European way of thinking that is now broadly defined as the Enlightenment. Reason, which had previously been considered a useful tool, was now celebrated as the power by which we can understand the universe and improve the human condition. The Enlightenment brought enormous progress in science, technology and medicine, but within it were the seeds of its own destruction. Revelation was made subject to reason.

This turn-around was to have a huge effect on people's response to Christianity. However, most ordinary people in the eighteenth century were largely unaffected by such philosophical wranglings. The secularization of Western society began in earnest throughout the nineteenth century, although the Victorian era was still powerfully influenced by Christian ideas.

Then, in the twentieth century, the full implications of the Enlightenment started to be seen. Since revelation was subject to reason, the miracles of Scripture, and indeed the traditional concept of God, began to be explained rationally. The faith of a society was being eroded. The fruits of the seeds sown in earlier centuries were seen in a devastatingly clear light.

Now, in our own day, many are questioning the suppositions of the Enlightenment. We can no longer be described as a secular society—we live in an age that is the most religious for several generations. It is also an age of "new spirituality." Rising up out of this shift of thinking, many are resisting rationalism. It has highlighted well the emptiness and shortcomings of rationalism and materialism. The "new spirituality" emphasises experience and values spirituality, but it goes further than this.

What is the new spirituality?

Bishop Graham Cray has described Western culture as a "pick-and-mix culture." What we have called "new spirituality" is an umbrella term that covers various diverse and disparate movements with a seemingly limitless array of disconnected beliefs and lifestyles. Sometimes people are committed to a particular path, while at other times it is more a matter of dabbling in whatever works for a certain individual. It is almost impossible to define because it has so many different branches. It has no leader, no organization, no structure, and no headquarters. It is a groundswell, an uncentralized movement of many diverse constituents. Caryl Matrisciana, looking back on her experience of many years involved in the New Age movement, for example, describes it as being like the recipe for a cake:

2 cups of hope (carefully sift out all fear)

2 cups of altered consciousness (Yoga, drugs, or meditation to taste)

3 tablespoons each of self-awareness, self-improvement and self-esteem (be sure to melt away anything negative)

1 heaped teaspoon of peace

1 large dollop of love

1 generous pinch each of humanism, Eastern mysticism and occultism

1 handful of holism

1 scoop of mystical experience.

Mix thoroughly together. Bake in a warm, friendly environment. Fill with your most appealing dreams. Garnish generously with positive thoughts and good vibrations.[3]

On the surface, parts of this new spirituality are either good or harmless. It often comes in the guise of self-help programs, holistic health, a concern for world peace, ecology, and spiritual enlightenment. Indeed, by themselves, certain elements such as the stress on good nutrition, the avoidance of drugs and respect for creation find an ally in Christianity. However, often under the sugar coating there is a dangerous pill. As St. Paul warns us, "Satan himself masquerades as an angel of light" (2 Corinthians 11:14).

First, it is often a mixture of Eastern mysticism and other practices that have been given a Western materialistic flavor. Hindu and Buddhist doctrines have been adapted for the Western world. A string of gurus has blended Eastern concepts with a Western thirst for fulfilment, expression, and enlightenment. There is a great deal of teaching on karma and Zen.

Second, there is the influence of nature religions from around the world, including the folk beliefs of American Indians and Wicca witchcraft.

Third, there are a number of practices that are overtly occult in nature. Astrology, horoscopes, fortune-telling, clairvoyance, consulting the dead, spiritism, mediums, channelling, spirit guides, and tarot cards are all widely used. All practices such as these are condemned in the Bible: "Let no one be found among you who sacrifices their son or daughter in the fire, who practices divination or sorcery, interprets omens, engages in witchcraft, or casts spells, or who is a medium or spiritist or who consults the dead. Anyone who does these things is detestable to the LORD" (Deuteronomy 18:10–12). These warnings are reiterated elsewhere in the Bible (Leviticus 19:26, 31; Galatians 5:20; Revelation 9:20–21).

The influence of the movement has been very significant, sometimes in particular within celebrity culture. Among many other movements, Kabbalah is a current fascination of many. Eitan Yardeni, who has given one-on-one instruction to Madonna, Demi Moore, and Roseanne Bar, suggested in an interview that such practices help celebrities deal with stardom:

> The rule in Kabbalah is that the more a person has, the more they need to
> work on themselves, in every area . . . With that power of having so much
> comes a greater challenge, a great amount of work to become humble about
> it. It's a struggle, to have so much . . . With celebrities, at least those who
> are honest with themselves and ready to do the spiritual work, they realize

that fame is not enough. The test is to realize that the temporary glitz, the temporary high, the temporary fame, is not true power. If you let the power control you, you'll be miserable. That's just the truth.[4]

What are the beliefs of "new spirituality"?

The "new spirituality" is both diverse and disparate, making it hard to summarize its beliefs. Generally, however, the ideals include being connected to the energy of creation, but spirituality doesn't necessarily mean having a religious context. Spirituality is seen as being what and who people are. These strands of thought illustrate a vision of the world which late theologian John Stott describes in what he calls "three pithy sayings": "All is God," "All is one," and "All is well."[5]

The first, "All is God," is generally known as pantheism. God is in everything. He is de-personified. He is an impersonal energy, a creative force. A god-like force runs through all creation: trees, animals, rocks, and people. In many strands of thinking in "new spirituality," there is no distinction between the creator and what He has created. The earth is divine, as are the stars and planets. This sometimes leads to a return to the pagan worship of Mother Earth and to the belief that the stars and planets and even crystals have power and influence.

In the New Age movement, there is no God outside His creation. God lies within each of us, and we are each a part of God. Actress and prominent New Age advocate Shirley Maclaine states that "Everyone is God. Everyone." Similarly, Eckhart Tolle writes:

> Identification with your mind creates an opaque screen of concepts, labels, images, words, judgments, and definitions that blocks all true relationship. It comes between you and yourself, between you and your fellow man and woman, between you and nature, between you and God. It is this screen of thought that creates the illusion of separateness, the illusion that there is you and a totally separate "other." You then forget the essential fact that, underneath the level of physical appearances and separate forms, you are one with all that is.[6]

The way to find God is to look within. Hence the title of one of Shirley Maclaine's books is *Going Within*. Swami Muktananda says, "Kneel to your own self. Honor and worship your own being. God dwells within you as you." In a UK television interview with Michael Parkinson, the British novelist and comedy scriptwriter Ben Elton commented, "I think it's fairly well accepted that we live in a post-faith age . . . but people still need faith and they find it in all sorts of ways. God famously made man in his image but now I think we make God in man's image. People choose a religion: 'the God of my choice.'"

Choosing our own God like this can seem very attractive, but ultimately it cannot fulfil the "need" that Elton speaks about. G. K. Chesterton highlighted the problems in 1908 in his book *Orthodoxy*: "Of all conceivable forms of enlightenment the worst is what . . . people call the inner-light. Of all horrible religions the most horrible is the god within. That Jones shall worship the God within him turns out ultimately to mean that Jones shall worship Jones." Humankind has fallen once again for the primeval temptation: "you will be like God" (Genesis 3:5).

Although there is a great deal of talk about compassion and love, the "new spirituality" movement is often self-centered. The starting point for change (with perhaps the long-term goal of helping others) is the development of the self. The worship of self manifests itself in books and courses on self-realization, self-fulfilment, self-help, self-confidence, self-improvement, self-worth, self-esteem, and self-love. The highest goal is to find one's own happiness, satisfaction, and success. To find one's own self is to find God.

This, of course, is an explicit assault on the self-denial at the heart of true Christianity. It is the opposite of the New Testament, where the way of fulfilment is loving and serving a personal God and loving and serving others. The way of fulfilment is not self-worship but self-denial, exemplified supremely in the life, death, and resurrection of Jesus Christ.

Second, "All is one," for which the technical term is "monism." The new spirituality is essentially syncretistic. It attempts to reconcile opposites and bring about a synthesis of all religions. In so doing, it rejects much orthodox Christianity, which is seen as rigid, structured, and narrow-minded.

Moral absolutes are often rejected: "sin" is not a popular word in the new spirituality, which thinks that our problem is not sin, but ignorance of our true self and true potential. This is solved by enlightenment, spiritual revelation, and education. For some, there is no objective standard of right and wrong. As one spiritual sage from India put it, when speaking to Caryl Matrisciana, "It's not a question of whether you are good or bad . . . good and bad are relative. They are two sides of one coin, part of the same whole."[7]

In a similar vein, Carl Frederick wrote in *est: Playing the Game the New Way*, "You are the Supreme being . . . there isn't any right or wrong." Shirley Maclaine's philosophy might be summed up as: "If it feels good, do it." The New Age offers the attraction of a spirituality without the cost of repentance. It is sometimes called "hippy values for a modern lifestyle."

Guidance comes from within. John W. Travis and Regina Sara Ryan in the *Wellness Workbook* write:

> So if love is as natural as breathing, and eating, and working and playing, it is as natural as "sexing." If love becomes our "life support system," then every decision we make, sex included, will be guided by it. We will choose to have sex with one another if it enhances our experience of unification with all that is.[8]

Since our problem is not sin but ignorance, there can be no judgment. In contrast to the Christian view that "people are destined to die once, and after that to face judgment" (Hebrews 9:27), some subscribe to a belief in reincarnation. Reincarnation is not always taught as cosmic justice, where we will be graded up or down depending on how good or bad we have been. Rather, everyone is eventually making progress onwards and upwards towards complete spiritual enlightenment and perfection. Again, they have fallen for Satan's lie: "You will not certainly die" (Genesis 3:4).

Monism ("All is one") is taken to even further extremes in some parts of the spirituality, in which there is no distinction made between God and Satan. Since all is one, the devil himself is worshipped.

The third saying with which John Stott summarizes the new spirituality is "All is well." Under this heading we can group the many and varied hopes new spiritualities offer for a better life and a better future for the world. The solution to many of the world's most complex problems are said to be "spiritual" solutions. As comedian and author Russell Brand wrote in *The Guardian* following the British riots of 2011:

> Young people have no sense of community because they haven't been given one. They have no stake in society . . . I don't know enough about politics to ponder a solution and my hands are sticky with blood money from representing corporate interests through film, television and commercials, venerating, through my endorsements and celebrity, products and a lifestyle that contributes to the alienation of an increasingly dissatisfied underclass. But I know, as we all intuitively know, the solution is all around us and it isn't political, it is spiritual. Gandhi said: "Be the change you want to see in the world."[9]

Once again, Christians can find an ally in this hope for a "spiritual" change in the most difficult issues facing societies today, but for very different reasons. For some this hope is incredibly expansive, and involves a new world order and a new world religion.

Jesus warned against such claims:

> For false messiahs and false prophets will appear and perform great signs and wonders to deceive, if possible, even the elect. See, I have told you ahead of time.
>
> "So if anyone tells you, 'There he is, out in the wilderness,' do not go out; or, 'Here he is, in the inner rooms,' do not believe it. For as lightning that comes from the east is visible even in the west, so will be the coming of the Son of Man."
>
> **Matthew 24:24–27**

What is wrong with the new spirituality?

The new spirituality is right to challenge the prevailing materialism and rationalism of our times. It is right to emphasize the importance of experience and to value spirituality. It is right to stress compassion, love and unity. Millions who are engaged in the new spirituality are on the right track in the sense that they are searching for spiritual reality. Yet these emphases fall way short of the glorious truths of Christianity.

We in the church are often to blame for having presented a form of Christianity that is hierarchical, structured, and narrow-minded. We can sympathize with David Icke when he wrote, "I feel the traditional Church as an organization has let down the world badly with its dogma and rigidity"[10] and with Oprah Winfrey when she writes of religion that is just doctrine without spirituality.[11]

The remedy lies not in the rejection of Christianity, but in a reappraisal of what is at the heart of the Christian faith. When we look at this, we see how far short the new spirituality movement falls of the glorious truth about the Trinitarian God of the orthodox Christian faith.

First, it does not get near the truth about God the Father. God is not an impersonal, abstract force, but the transcendent personal creator of the whole universe. And yet He is immanent. He wants to be in a relationship with us as human beings. We can speak to Him and He speaks to us. He is a Father who loves us and we are called to respond in love to Him and for our brothers and sisters. These are the glorious truths on which our Christian culture is built. The new spirituality will take us back to paganism, and St. Paul warns us against those who "exchanged the truth about God for a lie, and worshiped and served created things rather than the Creator" (Romans 1:25).

We were made to live in a relationship that involves the love and worship of God. As St. Augustine put it, "You have made us for yourself, and our heart is restless until it rests in you." That is why there is a restlessness within the new spirituality. There is a continual searching for an illusory peace. Shirley Maclaine writes: "Whenever I ask people what they want for themselves and for the world, the answer is almost always the same —peace."[12]

Sadly, this continual search can easily go awry. One woman in our congregation who was involved in the New Age for about three years told

me about her initial feeling of self-growth, and being set to "break the rules."
But soon she found she was imprisoned.

> I was like a lamb to the slaughter. It was like being on drugs. I was constantly
> looking for bigger experiences. I went on more and more expensive courses.
> I felt I was going out of my mind. It leaves you stuck in a place you don't
> understand—where you can't relate to the world. It led me away from
> anything good and nourishing. You just don't know when you are going to
> be healed.

She eventually found fulfilment, peace, and healing in a relationship with
God the Father, who alone can bring true and lasting peace.

Second, the new spirituality does not get near the truth about God the
Son. Jesus is seen as one of the ascended masters, along with Buddha,
Krishna, and others. Extraordinary rewritings of the New Testament Gospel
accounts abound. Shirley Maclaine has even claimed that Jesus was a
member of the Essenes, whose "teachings, principles, values and priorities
in life were so similar to those of the so-called New Age today . . . Christ
demonstrated what we would today call precognition . . . levitation, telepathy
and occult healing."[13]

David Icke claims that between the ages of twelve and thirty "Jesus
travelled widely to countries like India, Greece, Turkey, Egypt, France and
England . . . He once had to self-heal himself after contracting tuberculosis."
According to Icke, his disciples were "all Planetary Devas." After his death
on the cross "friends buried the body in a cellar and it has never been
found."[14] However ingenious these suggestions might be, there is absolutely
no historical evidence to support any of them.

At the most extreme end, the Bhagwan Shree Rajneesh bought a town in
America and set up his own Ashram where his Western disciples underwent
enlightenment therapy, which put emphasis on sex, drugs, and violence. The
net gain to the Bhagwan was a garage full of ninety-three Rolls Royces. Jesus
was rich, but for our sakes became poor so that we might become rich. The
Bhagwan was poor, but became rich and in doing so left a lot of others very
poor.

In trying to accommodate Jesus into the new spirituality, adherents miss out on the glorious truth of Jesus Christ, that he is "the way and the truth and the life" (John 14:6). He was, and is, God made man for our salvation. In His great love, Jesus died on the cross for us, in order to free us from guilt, addiction, fear, and death. He made forgiveness possible, bringing us friendship with God, the experience of His love and the power to change.

Consequently, He liberates us to love and serve others and to become more like Jesus Himself. These things are at the heart of the biblical understanding of salvation. This salvation is not something we could ever earn or achieve ourselves; it is a free gift from God. The only salvation in the new spirituality is self-salvation and the only forgiveness is self-forgiveness. In *A Course in Miracles*,[15] a typical workbook used by many in the New Age movement for daily reading, lesson 70 is headed "My salvation comes from me." The reader is urged to repeat, "My salvation comes from me. It cannot come from anywhere else." On the contrary, the New Testament asserts that Jesus is the only way of salvation (Acts 4:12). The new spirituality misses out on this wonderful news.

They miss out too on the good news of his resurrection. British church leader Michael Green writes:

Our destiny is not to go through many purgative reincarnations until the grossness of our lives is melted away, but after death to share in the resurrection life of which the Easter Jesus is the pledge. "To depart is to be with Christ, which is far better."

"We shall be like him, when we see him as he is." That is the conviction of those who knew him. Is it beyond belief? Not reincarnation, based on karma,

but resurrection, based on the cross and resurrection of Jesus, which points
both to our forgiveness and to our destiny. A totally different world view.
And one which challenges us to make up our minds, and choose.[16]

Third, new spirituality does not get near the truth about God the Holy
Spirit. In the new spirituality we see a search for spiritual power, spiritual
experience, and transformed lives. There is no greater spiritual power than
the power of the Holy Spirit, no greater experience than the fullness of the
Holy Spirit, and no more effective power to transform our lives.

One woman told me how she had tried Buddhism, Zen, Hinduism,
transcendental meditation, the occult, and all kinds of other practices.
Then one day she read Jackie Pullinger's book *Chasing the Dragon*, about
her work among drug addicts in Hong Kong. She went out there and saw
people being set free and healed by the power of the Holy Spirit. She
saw the life, love, joy, and peace the Holy Spirit brought to people's lives.
I asked her what the difference was between that and her experiences in
the New Age. She replied that she had seen real power in both, but added,
"One power, the New Age power, meant opting out of society, whereas
the power of the Holy Spirit meant opting back into society and changing
people's lives."

It is interesting that at a time of great outpouring of the power and
gifts of the Holy Spirit in the worldwide church (which began at the turn
of the century) we are seeing what appears to be a satanic counterfeit
(which began shortly afterwards). But Satan cannot counterfeit holiness.
The Holy Spirit transforms Christians into the likeness of Jesus Christ
(2 Corinthians 3:18). The fruit of the Spirit is love, joy, peace, patience, kindness, goodness, faithfulness, gentleness, and self-control (Galatians 5:22–23).

What are we to do?

First, there is a need for a double repentance. On the one hand, if we
have been involved in any way in practices of the new spirituality, whether
unwittingly or not, we need to recognize that they are wrong and to ask
God's forgiveness and turn away from all such things. We need to turn to
Jesus Christ who died on the cross so that we could be forgiven. We need
to ask the Holy Spirit to come and live within us.

On the other hand, those of us who have been involved in the church need to repent of our rigidity, rationalism, and failure to make the church relevant to the culture in which we live. We should also acknowledge where new spirituality has properly challenged our own prejudices. The interest in holistic medicine, for example, does in some senses move us back towards a true Christian understanding of the human being as one, rather than making a distinction between body and soul.

Second, we need to soak ourselves in the truth. Paul warns us: "See to it that no one takes you captive through hollow and deceptive philosophy" (Colossians 2:8) and again in Timothy:

> For the time will come when people will not put up with sound doctrine. Instead, to suit their own desires, they will gather around them a great number of teachers to say what their itching ears want to hear. They will turn their ears away from the truth and turn aside to myths. But you, keep your head in all situations.
> **2 Timothy 4:3-5**

We don't need to read lots of books about new spirituality. The way to spot a counterfeit is to know the real thing really well. Caryl Matrisciana uses a helpful analogy:

> "Mum's been working at the bank for over a year," my friend Chris told me. "And she's been getting the most amazing education."
>
> "What do you mean?"
>
> "She's learning all about money."
>
> "I guess she'd have to know about money if she's going to work in a bank!" I laughed.
>
> Chris smiled. "I mean she's really learning about money. They are teaching her to know the color of each bill, the size of it, even the way it's water-marked. They are showing her the details of the inks and papers."
>
> "How do they teach her?"
>
> "Well, they just keep having her handle it. They point out all the various things they want her to remember. But they figure the more she works with money, feels it, counts it, and stacks it, the more familiar it'll be to her."

"That makes sense, I suppose. But what's the point?"

"Here's the point. Yesterday they blindfolded her. They slipped a couple of counterfeit bills in her stack of money. She picked them out by touch!"

"So she's studying counterfeit money too, then?"

"No . . . that's just it. The people at the bank know that a person doesn't need to study the counterfeits."

"I see. But it seems as if they're going to a lot of trouble, doesn't it?"

"Not really. The banks know that the counterfeits are getting better and better, more and more sophisticated. And it's been proved a thousand times over that *if a bank teller knows the real money extremely well, he can't be fooled by the counterfeits.*"[17]

Third, we need to bring the good news of Jesus to those who are involved in the new spirituality. On the whole, those involved are simply people searching for the truth. They recognize that materialism does not satisfy. They recognize the limits of reason. They are seeking an experience of the spiritual. We need to demonstrate by our lives the supernatural power of God: Father, Son, and Holy Spirit.

CHAPTER 5

DOES RELIGION DO MORE HARM THAN GOOD?

At Holy Trinity Brompton church in London, we pray for various groups in the congregation who work in different sectors. I recall a time when we met to pray for those involved in British politics, government, and public life. Among the group were four Members of Parliament, two senior police officers, and many others working within the police, the Foreign Office, and the Civil Service. Speaking with this group afterwards, it became evident that these Christians had concerns about their place in contemporary public life. A member of the Civil Service told of how his colleague, a man in a senior position, was an active member of the British Humanist Society. The colleague believes people of faith should be kept out of the Civil Service, since their views and decisions would be negatively affected by their beliefs. This man had recently been placed on the recruitment committee.

Many people experience similar antipathy towards faith in public life, whether at school or university, or in various professions. A number of people have said that in education, the judiciary, and the medical profession—roles that comprise elements of influence, care, or vulnerability—there are certain situations in which it has become extremely difficult to be a Christian today.

Tobias Jones, writing in *The Guardian*, said, "Until a few years ago religion was similar to soft drugs: a blind eye was turned to private use, but woe betide you if you were caught dealing."[1] That mood is changing. No longer is it assumed that the church is a good thing—a benefit to the society—whether or not others believe in the faith of that church. Perhaps for the first time since Constantine (AD 272-337), Christianity in the West is on the back foot.

One of Richard Dawkins' documentaries about religion was entitled *The Root of all Evil*. In it, the prominent atheist suggests that, far from making people better or doing good things in society, "faith is one of the world's great evils," and he describes the God of the Bible as an "evil monster." He is not alone in this view. Peter Watson, author of a recent book on the history of invention, was asked by the *New York Times* to name humanity's worst invention. He answered, "Without question, ethical monotheism . . . This has been responsible for most of the wars and bigotry in history." So, how do Christians respond to the charge that religion does more harm than good in society?

First, Christians should acknowledge that actions carried out in the name of Jesus have sometimes caused considerable harm. The Crusades of the Middle Ages and the European religious wars of the sixteenth century are just two examples of times when religious zeal has caused great harm to many people. But the harm caused by groups of Christians at some periods of history should not lead us to regard the entirety of Christianity as intrinsically harmful to society. Though these acts were carried out in the name of Christ, it is right to ask whether they were in line with the teachings of Christ Himself. The answer is resolutely "no." Christ has taught His followers to turn the other cheek (Luke 6:29) and, when conflict broke out between His followers and those who opposed Him, He stopped the fighting and even healed the wounded enemy (Luke 22:51). Their actions were not in keeping with those of Christ.

Leading scientist Francis Collins writes that, when it comes to "the hypocritical behavior of those who profess belief . . . [we need to] keep in mind that the pure water of spiritual truth is carried in those rusty containers called human beings."[2]

The God of the Bible

Today's critics of religion are not the first to suggest that the God of the Bible is an "evil monster." In 1795, Thomas Paine wrote in *Age of Reason*:

> Whenever we read . . . the cruel and tortuous executions, the unrelenting vindictiveness with which more than half the Bible is filled, it would be more consistent that we call it the word of a demon than the word of God. It is a history of wickedness that has served to corrupt and brutalise humankind and for my own part, I sincerely detest it, as I detest everything that is cruel.[3]

How do we respond to this? We might consider three points in brief.

Examine the evidence of the whole Bible

Critics of the Bible are extremely selective in the passages of the Bible upon which they base their description of God. Any reader of the Bible will struggle to comprehend how Israel's actions in attacking surrounding nations served the justice of God. And yet, these same parts of the Old Testament also maintain that God is incredibly merciful and compassionate. When Abraham intercedes with God on behalf of the nations (Genesis 18), he finds that God will pardon the wickedness of the city for the sake of just a few good men and women. Similarly, in the middle of the narrative recounting how God broke Israel free from the oppressive hand of the Egyptian nation, even though the focus is on the just punishment of human wickedness, Moses still finds time to declare the goodness of God:

> "The LORD, the LORD, the compassionate and gracious God, slow to anger, abounding in love and faithfulness, maintaining love to thousands, and forgiving wickedness, rebellion and sin."
> **Exodus 34:6-7**

Likewise, the prophetic literature focuses on God as one who is supremely concerned about social justice and caring for the poor. Through Zechariah, for example, God says:

> "This is what the LORD Almighty said: 'Administer true justice; show mercy and compassion to one another. Do not oppress the widow or the fatherless, the foreigner or the poor.'"
> **Zechariah 7:9–10**

It will always be possible to cherry-pick extreme examples, taking them out of context in order to build up a horrible picture of God as an "evil monster." Nevertheless, the Bible demands to be read as a whole. It paints a picture of a loving and good God. While we struggle to understand how some of the events the Bible recounts fit within that picture of God, we should not let them obscure the rest.

I have endeavored to read the whole Bible every year since I have been a Christian (over thirty-five years), and I simply do not recognize the God that Thomas Paine and the New Atheists describe. I certainly do not believe in the God they describe; the God I know is totally different. He is a God of love, whose love for us is as high as the heavens are above the earth, whose compassion is like that of a parent caring for His children. He is a God of justice and love, a God of kindness and compassion, and a God of mercy and grace (Psalm 103:11–13).

Read the Bible through the lens of Jesus

The Bible is meant to be read in the context of a living relationship with the God who is its central character. Reading the Bible is not an academic exercise but the expression of a relationship. Faith is about putting our trust in the God who speaks to us through His Word. God has revealed Himself in the Bible. It is possible, as Jesus said, to hold to the Scriptures, but not read them in the context of this life-giving relationship: "You study the Scriptures diligently because you think that in them you have eternal life. These are the very Scriptures that testify about me," (John 5:39).

As Christians, we believe that Jesus is the image of the invisible God; Jesus said, "Anyone who has seen me has seen the Father" (John 14:9). In Luke 24:27, we read that "beginning with Moses and all the Prophets, he

[Jesus] explained to them what was said in all the Scriptures concerning himself." By looking at the Scriptures through the lens of Jesus, the Old Testament turns into a Christian text. We have to look at the Old Testament through the life, character, death, and resurrection of Jesus. For example, we might consider Jesus' death: Jesus did not do violence, but He allowed violence to be done to Him; He gave His life as a ransom on our behalf. Many passages in the Old Testament change shape when considered in this way.

We also need to look at the Scriptures through the lens of Jesus' teaching. Jesus said, "Do to others as you would have them do to you" (Luke 6:31); "Love your neighbor as yourself" (Matthew 22:39); "Love your enemies and pray for those who persecute you" (Matthew 5:44). Again, we should interpret the Old Testament through this lens.

Recognize the positive impact of the Bible

We should remember that Jesus' teaching is pivotal in the history of Western civilization. It has provided a moral code: an absolute right and an absolute wrong; an absolute good, and an absolute evil. If the God of the Bible is to be dismissed, the moral code will be turned on its head. Or it will need a new basis, if there can be one.

The Bible itself has formed the historic basis for society's understanding of what good and evil are. If that basis is to be done away with, and God written off as an "evil monster," questions must be asked about what moral path society will follow. In this regard, what little those making the charge have to offer as alternatives is troubling to say the least. If we are just a product of our genes and our environment, or if we are dancing to the tune of our DNA,[4] then there is no place for absolute standards of morality, which become purely subjective. Rod Liddle wrote in the Sunday Times:

> Nowhere though do atheists flail more ineffectually than in attempting to fill what Sartre called the "God-shaped Hole" inside all of us: our need to believe in something from which we derive our notion of morality. Dawkins acknowledges this need for something and concocts 10 commandments. In place of don't kill, steal or covet your neighbor's wife, he has things like, "Value the future on a timescale longer than your own," or, "Enjoy your own sex life (so long as it damages nobody else)." It is the 10 Commandments

handed down . . . not in stone but perhaps on organic tofu. It is beyond parody, and its potential longevity as a useful moral code can be counted in years rather than millenniums.[5]

When the absolute standard is removed, all that remains is utilitarianism; and utilitarian ethics have worrying implications. In the afterword to John Brockman's book *What is Your Dangerous Idea?* Dawkins wrote this on the subject of eugenics:

> I wonder whether, some sixty years after Hitler's death, we might at least venture to ask what the moral difference is between breeding for musical ability and forcing a child to take music lessons. Or why it is acceptable to train fast runners and high jumpers and not to breed them . . . hasn't the time come when we should stop being frightened to ask the question?
> . . . It is harder than most people realize to justify the unique and exclusive status that *Homo sapiens* enjoys in our unconscious assumptions. Why does "pro life" always mean "pro human life?" Why are so many people outraged at the idea of killing an eight-celled human conceptus while cheerfully masticating a steak that cost the life of an adult, sentient, and probably terrified cow?[6]

Dawkins thus implies that there is no absolute reason to prefer people to cows. Hitchens too often refers to people as mammals. Yet if human beings are not distinguished from animals, the sanctity of human life is abandoned in favor of principles such as, "It is wrong to reduce the amount of worthwhile life."

Recently I saw an item on the news about Sister Frances Dominica, who won the Woman of the Year Award in 2007. Sister Frances started Helen House, which cares for very sick and dying children in Oxfordshire, England, providing practical and

"Is having to go to Church a form of tyranny?"

spiritual support for parents and families trying to look after such children at home. It is deeply moving to see Sister Frances and the people who work at Helen House caring for these children with life-threatening and terminal illnesses, in the most loving way, giving them the best possible life for their very short period on this earth. It begs the question, "Why do they do it?" They do it because they believe in the God of the Bible and in the sanctity of human life: that every child, however disabled, is made in the image of God and is loved by and precious to Him. The God of the Bible as revealed in Jesus Christ is not an evil monster but the only hope for the future of our civilization.

Is faith really "one of the world's great evils"?

Faith has been described as "one of the world's great evils, comparable to the smallpox virus but harder to eradicate."[7] Let us consider three aspects of this belief.

Distinguish between faith and the misuse of faith

As we saw above, the Crusades represented a *misuse* of the Christian faith. It is imperative for both those of faith and none to distinguish between the use and misuse of their beliefs. The leading atheists focus only on the *misuse* of faith, never on its use for good. However, in contrast, when it comes to secular ideologies, they focus only on their use for good, never on misuse. Paul Copan writes:

> Much of the blood shed in the 20th century was the result of atheist ideologues. It's ironic that religion gets the blame for violence, but critics of religion are silent when a secular or atheistic faith—such as that of Stalin or Mao Tse-tung—wreaks utter destruction on millions upon millions of lives.[8]

Even the advances of modern science can be abused, as the development of napalm, landmines, and gas chambers shows. In the same way, faith can be abused through its *misuse*. As Canon David Watson often used to say, "The opposite of misuse is not disuse, it is right use." This is a reflection echoed by the Northern Irish Christian writer John Lennox, who has experienced at first hand the harm religious conflict and the misuse of faith can bring:

As a Northern Irishman, I am all too familiar with a certain brand of sectarian violence where a religious history has been used to fan the flames of terrorism (on both sides of the divide); although, as historians point out, a whole additional complex of political and social factors has been at work that makes analysis in terms of religion alone far too simplistic. What, then, have I to say about this evil aspect of religion?

The first thing to say is that I roundly condemn and abhor it, every bit as much as the New Atheists. I do so, be it noted, as a Christian. For, although the New Atheists' charge against Christendom for its violence may well be justified, their charge is not valid against the teaching of Christ himself . . . People who engage in violent and cruel activities at any time, in Northern Ireland or the Balkans or anywhere else, while invoking the name of God, are certainly *not* obeying Christ when they do so, whatever they may say to the contrary. After all, the name "Christian" means a disciple or follower of Jesus Christ. Following Christ means obeying his commandments. And one of those commands was the explicit *prohibition* of the use of force to defend Christ or his message . . . So let it be said loudly and clearly—it will have to be loud to be heard above the caterwauling of the New Atheists—*Christ repudiated violence*. He would not allow force to be used to save him from false accusation, suffering, and even death.[9]

Remember the harm done in the name of atheism

The premise of the New Atheism is that the world would be vastly improved if only we could get rid of religion. The acclaimed journalist John Humphrys writes that "for atheists to claim that without religion peace and harmony would reign is patently absurd. It's not the Bible that proves that. It's the history books."[10] Keith Ward, formerly of Oxford University, points out what we saw above—that, "The two world wars were not fought on religious grounds at all . . . there were no religious doctrines or practices at issue in those wars. The most terrible conflicts in human history were not religious."[11]

Evil things *have* been done in the name of atheism. Humphrys reminds us that this includes terrorism itself—despite its frequent association with religion. The British political philosopher John Gray makes the point that, "It is easy to forget how during the twentieth century terror was used on a vast scale by secular regimes . . . 'The roots of contemporary terrorism are in radical Western ideology—especially Leninism—far more than in religion.'"[12] It is estimated that, in the USSR, twenty million were killed; in China: sixty-five million; in North Korea: two million and in Cambodia: two million.

At least some of this terrorism was carried out by atheistic regimes *against* people of faith and religion itself. It is estimated that the total number of people killed by Communist governments through the extermination of their own population and carrying out explicitly antireligious policies is somewhere between eighty-five and one hundred million. John Cornwell, Fellow of Jesus College, Cambridge, points out that, "Stalin's atheism, moreover, was a crucial feature of his entire ideology. He oppressed, imprisoned, murdered [Christians], destroying their . . . churches throughout the length and breadth of Russia."[13] In a speech given on 18 November 1961, Krushchev, who led the Soviet Union at that time, outlined their philosophy, saying, "We need a considered and well balanced system of scientific atheistic education which would embrace all strata and groups of the population and prevent the spread of religious views especially among children and adolescents."[14]

Both Christianity and atheism have at times brought harm to our world. But harm comes about through *misuse*. Nobody is suggesting that all atheists do terrible things. My father was an atheist (or, at least, an agnostic), and he was a wonderful man, one of the heroes of my life.

Appreciate the good done in the name of Jesus

While Christians have done harm in history, it is not true that the church has consistently done more harm than good. Author and theologian Jonathan Hill acknowledges that much that has been done in the name of Christianity has been bad but warns us to acknowledge that this does not define Christianity as a whole:

> The Christian churches, like any other social institution, have a very complex history and make-up. Clearly, they've not been simply shining beacons of goodness, and I wouldn't wish to pretend that they have. But by the same token, they've not been simply terrible sources of evil either . . .[15]

Unfortunately, the critics of Christianity fixate so much upon the bad that they do not see that the church has always strived imperfectly to be a source of blessing. One example is the remarkable achievement of Christians in establishing hospitals throughout Europe. The Christians of the Middle Ages were unique in establishing leper colonies, caring for those whom other societies "banished from all human habitations." Christians have been establishing hospitals and centers of care since the days of the Roman empire. There was no precedent for this act of love and care in the pagan society out of which it emerged.

When the plague hit the Greek city of Edessa, St. Ephraim (AD 306-73) established a hospital there to care for the afflicted. St. Basil the Great (AD 329-79) established a leper colony in Cappadocia. In Constantinople, rich members of the laity served the poor, bathed the sick, and gave alms for centuries. Indeed, these acts of charity were never more extensive than in the Middle Ages themselves, when the Crusades also took place. During this time the Benedictine monks alone were responsible for 2,000 hospitals in Western Europe. Such centers fed the hungry, cared for widows and orphans, and distributed alms. Increasingly, these centers of medical care also became centers of training, and so provided the forerunner to today's network of medical care and training.

Christianity, it must therefore be said, has also done a great deal of good in society. Theologian and philosopher David Bentley Hart suggests that, more often, historians looking closely at the Middle Ages with all the horrors of the Crusades see "a society that, for all its brutalities, mixed motives and inconstancies, was in some genuine way constructed around a central ideal of Christian love."[16]

Over the centuries, millions of ordinary Christians around the world have done good. Even people who are not Christians themselves recognize the good that is being done in the name of Jesus. John Humphrys is an agnostic and describes himself as a "failed atheist." After his program on Radio 4 *In Search of God* he received hundreds of letters in response to his search.

He writes:

For every skeptic, there were dozens of believers who said they had been converted by a specific event or experience . . . They are overwhelmingly sincere people who, one way or another, had found belief in God and that belief has changed their lives . . . most of the writers strike me as intelligent, discriminating people who have given a lot of thought to their faith, asked a lot of questions and usually managed to satisfy their doubts . . . . For every fanatic there are countless ordinary, decent people who believe in . . . God and wish no harm to anyone. Many of them regard it as their duty to try to make the world a better place.[17]

In a radio interview some time before his death, author and prominent atheist Christopher Hitchens said, "There is nothing that someone of faith can do that someone without can't do; there are no benefits that a Christian can make to society that a secular person can't also achieve." After listening to the radio program, Charlie Mackesy, the artist and sculptor, wrote down the response that he would have given, had he been at the interview:

All I can say, and I can only speak for myself, Christopher, is that there are things with faith in Jesus that I've done that I'd never have had the courage to do, ever; never had the patience to do; never had the love and the freedom to do; never had the inspiration or the guts to do; and never had the desire to do. I'm sure others without faith could achieve more, much more, but for me, without it, I would never have tried or attempted and failed, sometimes half of it. Jesus brings life and guts and courage into everything, for me.[18]

Christians do not claim to be better than those who are not; simply better than who they would have been, had they not become Christians. The gospel, the good news of Jesus, brings freedom and liberation to our lives, and the Holy Spirit transforms us from within. "The fruit of the Spirit is love, joy, peace, patience, kindness, goodness, faithfulness, gentleness and self-control" (Galatians 5:22-23). We see this fruit in the lives of people who follow Jesus, in their desire to care for the poor, visit the prisons, and care for the dying. Can it really be said that religion is one of the world's great evils?

Conclusion

I used to be an atheist with very similar views, though they were, of course, not as developed as those of the New Atheists. Then I encountered Jesus Christ and discovered a relationship with Him: a relationship with the God of the Bible who is not an evil monster. I experienced God's amazing love poured into my heart by the Holy Spirit, which gave me a love for God and a love for other people. That was one of the experiences that led me to become a vicar, because I long for other people to experience that same love in their own lives. Over the years I have seen the impact of this faith on our marriage and family life, and I have seen the impact of Christian faith on other families in our church. I have watched its impact on the young children, the teenagers, the students, and young adults who have grown up in a community of faith.

I have also watched people coming to faith in Jesus in studying Alpha at HTB, and I have heard many more stories from all around the world. They tell of changed lives: people whose marriages have been restored, whose relationships with their parents or children have changed beyond recognition, people who have been set free from addiction, or who were in prison and have come to faith in Jesus. They speak about how their faith has changed them, and how they are now making a contribution to society. Some have started ministries caring for the poor, for the homeless, and for people with AIDS. Why? Because they have experienced faith in Jesus Christ.

The small things that individual people do—acts of forgiveness, acts of love, acts of service—can be multiplied to millions and millions; they happen every day and are not necessarily recorded or known about, other than by very few. I cannot speak for religion in general, but I can tell you because I have seen it with my own eyes, that faith in Jesus Christ does not do harm—it does an immeasurable amount of good—because we follow the one who "went around doing good" (Acts 10:38).

CHAPTER 6

IS THE TRINITY UNBIBLICAL, UNBELIEVABLE, AND IRRELEVANT?

The word "Trinity" is derived from the Latin word *Trinitas*, which is a theological term invented to describe a threefold unity. Christianity rests on the doctrine of the threefold reality, the tri-personality, of one God. The word "Trinity" does not appear in the Bible and therefore it is sometimes also suggested that the idea of the Trinity is unbiblical.

Others suggest it is unbelievable because it is incomprehensible. The Athanasian Creed[1] (c. AD 500) sums up the doctrine of the Trinity like this: ". . . that the Father is God, the Son is God and the Holy Ghost is God, and yet there are not three gods, but one God."

In Lewis Carroll's sequel to *Alice's Adventures in Wonderland, Alice through the Looking Glass*, the White Queen made a habit of believing six impossible things before breakfast. Many wonder whether as Christians we are required to do something similar with the doctrine of the Trinity.

Still others regard the doctrine as an irrelevance. They may believe it is true, but they do not think it is of great importance to their daily lives. Sermons on the Trinity are not exactly crowd-pullers.

Why should we believe in the Trinity? Is it biblical? Is it believable? Is it comprehensible? Is it relevant to our lives today?

Is it biblical?

As mentioned above, the word "Trinity" does not appear in the Bible. It was first used in its Greek form by an early Christian writer called Theophilus, Bishop of Antioch, in c. AD 180. But as Professor F. F. Bruce remarked, "Let us not be misled by the foolish argument that because the term 'Trinity' does not occur in the scriptures, the doctrine of the Trinity is therefore unscriptural."

Christianity arose out of Judaism, which was a monotheistic faith (Deuteronomy 6:4) in contrast to the polytheism of the nations that surrounded it. The New Testament itself affirms that there is only one God (John 5:44; Romans 3:30; 1 Timothy 1:17; James 2:19).

The early Christians were faced with two historical events which revolutionized their understanding of God. First, they were faced with the revelatory events of the life, death, and resurrection of Jesus. In the wake of these revelations, they came to see that something about Jesus pointed to Him being God Himself. They soon found themselves worshipping Jesus as God (for example, John 20:28) and yet they totally rejected the polytheistic pattern of Roman religion. Instead, they came to see Him as a man whose identity was God and yet who was not identical to God.

Second, they had an experience of the Holy Spirit that lifted them out of the realms of human experience—one of being caught up in a relationship within the Godhead. They realized that the Holy Spirit was identified with God and Jesus and yet was not identical to either. He was not the Father, nor the Son, but He was one of them. They came to believe in the deity of the Father, the deity of the Son, and the deity of the Holy Spirit. Yet they never surrendered the belief there was only one God.

We can see how John, for example, sets this out in his Gospel. He asserts, with the other New Testament writers, that there is only one God (John 5:44; 17:3). Yet, in the opening sentences of his Gospel, he introduces us to two distinct persons within the unity of the Godhead: "In the beginning was the Word, and the Word was with God, and the Word was God." As J. I. Packer of Regent College in Vancouver, puts it:

> The Word was a person in fellowship with God, and the Word was himself Personally and eternally divine . . . but this is not all that John means us to learn about the plurality of persons in the Godhead . . . Our Lord (in John's

gospel) now gives parallel teaching, to the effect that the divine Spirit is also
a person ... Thus John records our Lord's disclosure of the mystery of the
Trinity: three persons, and one God ...[2]

The concept of the Trinity permeates the pages of the New Testament.
Some would say that there are hints of this doctrine even in the Old
Testament, as far back as the very beginning in Genesis 1:1–3a. In verse 1 we
read of God the Creator. In verse 2, "The *Spirit* of God was hovering over
the waters." Verse 3 begins, "And God said . . ."–God created through his
Word. John, in his Gospel, tells us that the Word is none other than Jesus
himself (John 1:14). Thus, God the Father, God the Son, and God the Holy
Spirit were there at the very beginning.

In the New Testament we find several prayers and blessings that very
deliberately mention the Father, Son, and Spirit together. Baptism takes
place in the name (singular) of the Father and the Son and the Holy Spirit
(Matthew 28:19). Paul ends his second letter to the Corinthians with what
we now call "The Grace": "May the grace of the Lord Jesus Christ, and
the love of God, and the fellowship of the Holy Spirit be with you all" (2
Corinthians 13:14). While these two texts do not expressly state the doctrine
of the Trinity, they point strongly towards it.

Paul sees virtually every aspect of the Christian faith and life in trinitarian
terms. As the church leader and writer John Stott argued in commenting
on Ephesians 1, both halves of the chapter are "essentially trinitarian . . .
both are addressed to God the Father . . . both refer specifically to God's
work in and through Christ . . . both sections of the chapter allude–even if
obliquely–to the work of the Holy Spirit . . . Christian faith and Christian life
are both fundamentally trinitarian."[3]

In chapter 2 of the same letter, our relationship with God and prayer is
seen in trinitarian terms. We pray "to the Father," through Jesus, "by one
Spirit" (Ephesians 2:18–for more detailed exposition see *Questions of Life*,
chapter 5). In chapter 3, the filling of the Spirit is described in trinitarian terms,
as we shall see later in this chapter. In chapter 4, Christian unity is urged for
trinitarian reasons: "There is . . . one Spirit . . . one Lord . . . one God and Father of all" (Ephesians 4:4–6). In his ethical instruction in the second half of
Ephesians 4, as John Stott points out, "It is natural for him, in issuing his moral

instructions, to mention the three Persons of the Trinity. He tells us to 'copy God,' to 'learn Christ' and not to 'grieve the Holy Spirit.'"[4]

Finally, when he refers to our worship, Paul again speaks in trinitarian terms (Ephesians 5:18-20). "Once again the doctrine of the Trinity informs and directs our devotion. When we are filled with the Holy Spirit we give thanks to God our Father in the name of the Lord Jesus Christ."[5]

Nor is Ephesians the only place where Paul's trinitarian thinking emerges. In 1 Corinthians he describes the gifts of the Spirit in this way: "There are different kinds of gifts, but the same *Spirit* distributes them. There are different kinds of service, but the same *Lord*. There are different kinds of working, but in all of them and in everyone it is the same *God* at work." (1 Corinthians 12:4-6, italics mine).

In 2 Thessalonians, Paul speaks in trinitarian terms once more when he talks of taking the initiative and providing both the means and goal of salvation: "*God* chose you as firstfruits to be saved through the sanctifying work of *the Spirit* . . . that you might share in the glory of our *Lord Jesus Christ*." (2 Thessalonians 2:13-14, italics mine).

Finally, in Romans 8, Paul describes the believer's relationship with God in terms of Father, Son and Spirit together:

> The *Spirit* you received does not make you slaves, so that you live in fear again; rather, the Spirit you received brought about your adoption to sonship. And by him we cry, "*Abba, Father*." The Spirit himself testifies with our spirit that we are God's children. Now if we are children, then we are heirs—heirs of God and co-heirs with *Christ*, if indeed we share in his sufferings in order that we may also share in his glory."
> **Romans 8:15-17, italics mine**

For Paul, we call God Father along with Christ, in the power of the Spirit.

Paul is not the only trinitarian writer in the New Testament. For example, at the beginning of his first epistle, Peter describes the way we are chosen by God in trinitarian terms: "To God's elect . . . who have been chosen according to the foreknowledge of *God the Father*, through the sanctifying work of *the Spirit*, to be obedient to *Jesus Christ* and sprinkled with his blood" (1 Peter 1:1-2, italics mine).

In spite of these and many other similar passages in the New Testament, the Bible has no formal credal statement about the Trinity—the identity and relationships of the Father, Son and Spirit—that is set out like the Athanasian Creed we mentioned above. The early church originally simply experienced and reflected upon the reality of God as Father, Son, and Holy Spirit. It was only later that a coherent and systematic doctrine was defined in response to very different and dangerous views of the Trinity that were being offered.

On the one hand, for example, Arius (c. AD 250-336), who was excommunicated from the church for heresy, argued that Jesus was divine but that His divinity was only partial and derivative. The Father, Son, and Holy Spirit were three distinct beings. "The Three he envisages are entirely different beings, not sharing in any way the same nature or essence."[6] In the sixth century, Philoponus of Alexandria held that there are three gods, who are all of the same sort, and yet distinct and separate from each other. This theology amounts to polytheism.

At the other extreme, Sabellius reduced the Trinity to a unity with three modes of expression. Father, Son, and Holy Spirit were no more than symbolic names for one God in His different activities. Instead of three persons, there was one being who changed mask according to whether He was acting as Creator, Redeemer, or Sanctifier. There was one person with three names.

Against such heretical views, the council of Constantinople in AD 381, building on the council of Nicaea in AD 325, spoke of one God (one substance) and three persons. This view of the Trinity has been held by every orthodox church since that time. The traditional doctrine is summed up by the later Athanasian Creed:

> We worship one God in Trinity, and Trinity in Unity, neither confounding the Persons nor dividing the Divine Being. For there is one Person of the Father, another of the Son, and another of the Holy Spirit: but the Godhead of the Father, the Son, and the Holy Ghost is all one.

Is it believable?

Those who find the doctrine unbelievable because they think it is incomprehensible might point to some other words in the Athanasian

Creed: "The Father incomprehensible, The Son incomprehensible, and The Holy Ghost incomprehensible . . . Not three incomprehensibles . . . but . . . one incomprehensible." As the theologian Alister McGrath points out, many are sorely tempted to add, "The whole thing incomprehensible!" In fact "incomprehensible" does not mean "beyond our understanding," rather it "means that the Persons cannot be grasped or pinned down. They cannot be contained or limited by human beings."[7] Certainly, we have to concede that it is not an easy doctrine to understand. We are dealing here with the nature of God Himself, so it is not surprising that He stretches the limits of our understanding. One of the greatest theologians of the church, Augustine of Hippo (AD 354–430), wrote fifteen volumes on the Trinity, synthesizing and adding the finishing touches to the most profound and exact statements which have ever been made on the subject. Yet even he never plumbed the full depth of this doctrine. God cannot be put in a neat box and easily understood.

A preacher speaking on the Trinity asked the congregation at the end of his sermon, "Have I made it clear?" One man in the congregation said, "Yes," to which the preacher replied, "In that case you have got it wrong!" St. Augustine himself said, "If you can understand it, it's not God!" He did not mean that we could not or should not seek to understand it, otherwise he would not have written fifteen volumes on the subject. What he meant was that there will always be an element of mystery about God.

In that case one might ask, "Why bother to try to understand?" and, "Does it really matter?" The answer is that it does matter and we need to try and understand it as far as we can, because it is fundamental to the Christian faith. Our God is Trinity.

Many have sought human analogies to help us to understand the doctrine. David Prior, the vicar of St. Michael's, Chester Square in London wrote to *The Times* in June 1992 suggesting a novel analogy:

> Last Sunday I dragged myself away from watching the end of the Test match at Lord's in order to preach at our evening service on the theme of "What Christians believe about the Trinity." The last three balls I watched being bowled were by Ian Salisbury, England's exciting new spin bowler. The first was a leg-spinner, the second a top-spinner, the third a googly.
>
> I had been ferreting around for a helpful illustration of the Trinity—and

there it was: one person expressing himself in three different, but very similar ways. The leg-spinner's stock ball represents God the Father, who created us to "feel after him;" the top-spinner, which goes straight through, represents the direct activity of God the Son; the googly represents the surprising activity of God the Holy Spirit.[8]

In any case, David Prior's letter elicited two interesting replies. The first, from R. A. Morris, who wrote, "David Prior's trinitarian illustration will have to be called wide. It reflects a serious theological error, identified in the early church as the idea that one God merely acts in different ways at different times. Better stick to three stumps in one wicket."[9] The second, from Timothy Russ: "Perhaps David Prior should have been studying the fathers of the church rather than watching the cricket on Trinity Sunday, for he seems to have expressed very concisely the Sabellian heresy 'one person expressing himself in three different ways,' instead of three persons in one substance. My own anxiety as I dragged myself away from the screen was: "'Will there be anyone at all in church?'"[10]

This correspondence illustrates the difficulty in seeking to find an appropriate human analogy.

The most basic analogy is a triangle: three sides but one triangle. Slightly less crude is the shamrock leaf as suggested by St. Patrick. Each of the three portions of the leaf is an essential part of that leaf, but the leaf itself is greater than all its parts. In a similar way, Great Britain's Union Flag is made up of the combination of the flags of St. George, St. Andrew, and St. Patrick. Others point to the sun—its source, its heat and its light.

Perhaps a better illustration is that of the universe itself, being made up of space, time, and matter: space, with its length, breadth, and height; time, with its future, past, and present; matter, consisting of energy, motion, and phenomena.

John Eddison, in *Talking to Children*, uses the analogy of a book. A book exists in three different and distinct ways at once—in the mind of the author, on the shelf in the library, and in the imagination of the reader. Others use the analogy of a house. The architect (God the Father) can say, "It's my house." The purchaser (God the Son) can say, "It's my house." And the tenant (God the Spirit) can say, "It's my house."[11]

The difficulty with all these analogies is that they are impersonal. However, they are illustrative of God's threefold nature. Of course, ideally, an analogy of the Trinity should be personal. However, there are difficulties with such analogies. Some have used the parallel of a family with a father, mother, and child. This tends towards the heresy of Philoponus as it suggests three Gods and not one. On the other hand, the idea sometimes used of a father, who is a fireman most of the time, a soccer player on Saturday and a fisherman on Sunday evening, is Sabellian as it suggests one God with three modes of expression.

When we try to understand the Trinity, we always come up against three human limits. First, we face the limits of human language. The Austrian philosopher Ludwig Wittgenstein pointed out that human words are completely incapable of describing something as mundane as the aroma of coffee. How much more difficult it must be to describe God in human language.

Second, we face the limits of human intellect and understanding. "Our little intellectual systems find themselves groaning under the strain of trying to accommodate God."[12] In describing the Trinity we have to resort to paradox. As defined by the Concise Oxford English Dictionary, a paradox is a "seemingly absurd though perhaps actually well-founded statement." Scientist and theologian Alister McGrath gives an example of the paradox from the world of science:

> An example of this from the world of science concerns the nature of light. By the first decade of the twentieth century, it was clear that light behaved in a very strange way—sometimes it seemed to behave as if it was a wave, and sometimes as if it was a particle. It couldn't be both at once, and so the cry "contradiction!" was raised. How could it be two totally different things? But eventually, through the development of the Quantum Theory, it was found that this contradiction expressed a fundamental difficulty in grasping what

the nature of light really was. In other words, the contradiction did not arise on account of light, but on account of our difficulties in conceiving it.[13]

He goes on to show that the nature of light was such that two contradictory models had to be used to account for its behavior (with God we require three contradictory models).

> Most of us know what light is without needing to think about waves, particles or Quantum Theory. Light is what we need in order to see, to do our everyday business, to read and write. It is what comes out of the sun, and to a lesser extent from the moon. It is what we get when we switch on electric light bulbs or strip lighting. If we were physicists, we might want to think about light in much more detail and go into the full complexities of it —and so we might start talking about waves, particles and Quantum Theory. But we don't need to do this in order to make use of light or to recognize it when we see it.[14]

The fact that we cannot fully comprehend the Trinity does not mean that it does not make sense. When I switch on the television I do not understand how it works, but there is an explanation beyond the limits of my understanding and which does make sense.

Third, we face the limits of our finite world and finite human lives. C. S. Lewis uses the most helpful analogy I have come across. He writes:

> And now, for a few minutes, I must ask you to follow rather carefully. You know that in space you can move in three ways—to left or right, backwards or forwards, up or down. Every direction is either one of these three or a compromise between them. They are called the three Dimensions. Now notice this. If you are using only one dimension, you could draw only a straight line. If you are using two, you could draw a figure: say, a square. And a square is made up of four straight lines. Now a step further. If you have three dimensions, you can then build what we call a solid body: say, a cube—a thing like a dice or a lump of sugar. And a cube is made up of six squares.
>
> Do you see the point? A world of one dimension would be a straight line. In a two-dimensional world, you still get straight lines, but many lines make one figure. In a three-dimensional world, you still get figures but many figures

make one solid body. In other words, as you advance to more real and more complicated levels, you do not leave behind you the things you found on the simpler levels: you still have them, but combined in new ways —in ways you could not imagine if you knew only the simpler levels.

Now the Christian account of God involves just the same principle. The human level is a simple and rather empty level. On the human level one person is one being, and any two persons are two separate beings—just as, in two dimensions (say on a flat sheet of paper) one square is one figure, and any two squares are two separate figures. On the Divine level you still find personalities; but up there you find them combined in new ways which we, who do not live on that level, cannot imagine. In God's dimension, so to speak, you find a being who is three Persons while remaining one Being, just as a cube is six squares while remaining one cube. Of course we cannot fully conceive a Being like that: just as, if we were so made that we perceived only two dimensions in space we could never properly imagine a cube. But we can get a sort of faint notion of it. And when we do, we are then, for the first time in our lives, getting some positive idea, however faint, of something super-personal—something more than a person. It is something we could never have guessed, and yet, once we have been told, one almost feels one ought to have been able to guess it because it fits in so well with all the things we know already. You may ask, "If we cannot imagine a three-personal Being, what is the good of talking about Him?" Well, there isn't any good talking about Him. The thing that matters is being actually drawn into that three-personal life, and that may begin any time—to-night, if you like.[15]

Is it relevant?

The doctrine of the Trinity is highly relevant because it sheds light on the nature of God and His interaction with his creation.

First, the Trinity shows that God is self-sufficient. Some people might be tempted to think that God can only be God if He has a world to be God of. The Trinity tells us that God had no need to create outside of Himself in order to be who He is. Some people also assume that before creation God was somehow lonely. The Trinity shows us that the three persons of the Trinity existed before the creation of the universe in a perfect life of love and communication. God did not create the world or humanity because of any lack or need, but out of the overflow of the love and communication of the Father, Son, and Spirit.

Second, it tells us that

three essential models must be used if the full depth of the Christian experience and understanding of God is to be expressed adequately. No one picture, image or model of God is good enough—and these three models are essential if the basic outline of our Christian understanding of God is to be preserved. The first model is that of a transcendent God who lies beyond the world as its source and creator; the second is the human face of God, revealed in the person of Jesus Christ; the third is that of the immanent God who is present and active throughout his creation. The doctrine of the Trinity affirms that these three models combine to define the essential Christian insights into the God who raised Jesus Christ from the dead. None of them, taken on its own, is adequate to capture the richness of the Christian experience of God.[16]

Third, it is the triune God who meets our most fundamental psychological needs as human beings. An occupational therapist, trained in psychology in a humanist secular framework, told me that she had been taught that we all need three things. First, we need a point of reference. We need to know who we are, where we have come from, and where we are going. Second, we need a role model (who might be, for example, a therapist) and third, we need a facilitator to help us to get there (this might come from a counselor or from some group help). When this woman became a Christian she said she realized that God is our point of reference, Jesus is our role model and the Holy Spirit is our facilitator. She saw that the Trinity meets the deepest psychological needs of every human being.

Fourth, the doctrine of the Trinity is relevant in that it teaches us that there is an inherent threefoldness about every act of God's revelation. Again and again we see single doctrines expressed in threefold ways, showing both the oneness and threeness of God, and requiring us to think in trinitarian terms of the nature of God. In the New Testament, virtually every doctrine in experience—baptism, grace, salvation, election, ethics, worship, unity—is described in trinitarian terms. In order to understand God and every doctrine about God we need to think in this way.

I want to end by looking at one example in more detail. In Ephesians 3 Paul describes the fullness of the Spirit in trinitarian terms when he prays that the Ephesian Christians will be filled with the Spirit.

> For this reason I kneel before the Father, from whom every family in heaven
> and on earth derives its name. I pray that out of his glorious riches he may
> strengthen you with power through his *Spirit* in your inner being, so that
> *Christ* may dwell in your hearts through faith. And I pray that you, being
> rooted and established in love, may have power, together with all the Lord's
> holy people, to grasp how wide and long and high and deep is the love of
> Christ, and to know this love that surpasses knowledge—that you may be filled
> to the measure of all the fullness of *God*.
> **Ephesians 3:14-19, italics mine**

The fullness of the Spirit is an experience of the fatherhood of God. His prayer is to the Father who is the initiator of the process. In Romans 8 Paul speaks more explicitly of the involvement of the Father in the experience of the Spirit, "For those who are led by the Spirit of God are the children of God. The Spirit you received does not make you slaves, so that you live in fear again; rather, the Spirit you received brought about your adoption to sonship. And by him we cry, 'Abba, Father.' The Spirit himself testifies with our spirit that we are God's children." (Romans 8:14-16).

The fulness of the Spirit is also an experience of the love of Christ. He prays that "Christ may dwell in your hearts through faith. And I pray that you, being rooted and established in love, may have power, together with all the Lord's holy people, to grasp how wide and long and high and deep is the love of Christ, and to know this love that surpasses knowledge—that you may be filled to the measure of all the fulness of God" (Ephesians 3:17-19).

Finally, the fulness of the Spirit is an experience of the power of the Spirit. Paul prays that God would strengthen them "with power through his Spirit in your inner being" (verse 16). This is the power that Jesus promised to His disciples in His very last words before His ascension (Acts 1:8).

When the Holy Spirit fills us, we experience the Fatherhood of God, the love of Christ, and the power of the Spirit. Yet the three cannot be separated. He prays for "his Spirit," "Christ," and "all the fulness of God" to fill them. The three are in one and one in three. God is not meant only to be understood in our minds but also experienced in our hearts and lives. To be filled with the Spirit is to experience God as Trinity.

CHAPTER 7

IS FAITH IRRATIONAL?

As a former atheist, I used to think that faith was completely irrational. It was only when I encountered Jesus Christ that it made sense to me. People often ask the question: is there any evidence for the Christian faith? Or, as some suggest, is faith irrational by its very definition? The philosopher Friedrich Nietzsche famously wrote that faith "stands in opposition to all intellectual well-being."

Christianity must have an answer, not only to particular searching issues, but also to the question of whether faith itself is baseless and irrational. This chapter will consider the question of whether it is irrational by considering five preliminary points about faith itself.

It takes faith to believe there is no God

It is exceedingly difficult, perhaps even impossible, to *disprove* God's existence. Most philosophers and scientists agree that you cannot conclusively disprove the existence of God, because it is almost impossible to prove a "universal negative." In fact, even many atheists would concede that it is impossible to prove that God does not exist.

In 2009, a coalition of British Atheists ran an advertising campaign with the slogan "There *probably* is no God. Now stop worrying and enjoy your life" (italics mine). The word "probably" was included in recognition of the fact that it is impossible to prove the non-existence of God. This in itself is a belief. Atheists *believe* that there is no God.

It is not only religious people who believe things: *everyone depends on certain beliefs*. Christians have beliefs. Atheists have beliefs. Even agnostics have beliefs. A friend once told me this story:

Some time ago, during a slightly alcohol-assisted discussion on life, death and the origins of the universe, a friend turned to me and said, "You're a man of faith, what do you think?"

"We are all men and women of faith," I replied. "Some of us have faith that there is a God, some of us have faith that there is no God, and neither position is provable."

"Precisely," he said, "that's why I'm an agnostic."

"You don't escape either," I replied. "You just have faith that it's not important to decide."

Whether it is a question of God's existence, our worldview, or how we live, there is always an element of what we can call "faith," whatever we *believe*. Not believing in God typically means believing in something else.

Faith is an essential part of knowledge

There is an element of belief or faith to every area of knowledge. Albert Einstein once said:

> The mechanics of discovery are neither logical nor intellectual. It's a sudden illumination, almost a rapture. Later, to be sure, intelligence and analysis and experiment confirm (or invalidate) the intuition. But initially there is a great leap of imagination.[1]

Legal decisions may also require a step of faith. I practiced as a lawyer for a number of years and am very aware that when a jury brings a guilty verdict it is a step of faith. They do not know that the defendant is guilty, rather they must trust the witnesses and the evidence given. Every verdict involves an element of faith.

Indeed, human relationships themselves, which are universal, are based on a kind of faith. In September 2007, Ms. Yang, a twenty-six-year-old daughter of a former bricklayer, became China's richest person and the wealthiest woman in Asia when her father passed on all his wealth to her. Her fortune amounted to $16.2 billion. Asked by a Hong Kong newspaper why he had handed over his fortune to his daughter, Mr. Yang said, "Even if I reach the age of 100, I am going to give it to her anyway. She is family and I have *faith* in her."[2]

Faith is an important part of many aspects of life.

Faith and reason can be complementary

Faith involves belief and trust. Yet faith and reason do not by definition exclude each other; they can in fact be complementary. The Bible does not lead us towards a faith devoid of reason. Alongside the centrality of the heart and will, the New Testament also emphasises reason and the life of the mind.

Jesus said, "Love the Lord your God with all your heart and with all your soul and with all your *mind*" (Matthew 22:37, italics mine). Jesus himself said, "I am . . . the truth" (John 14:6). Likewise, when Paul was on trial accused of being insane, he said, "I am not insane . . . 'What I am saying is true and reasonable'" (Acts 26:25). Paul affirmed a rational basis for his belief in Jesus, and he often spoke about his "belief in the truth" (2 Thessalonians 2:13).

To be a Christian is to believe in the truth; there is rationality to faith. For this reason, the apostle Peter writes, "Always be prepared to give an answer to everyone who asks you to give the reason for the hope that you have" (1 Peter 3:15).

Faith is rational, but faith also goes beyond reason in the context of relationship. Take as an example my relationship with my wife, Pippa. If asked whether my love for my wife was rational or irrational, I would say that it is not irrational at all. There are very good reasons for it; there is lots of evidence on which I base my love for her. Yet to say that my love for her is *merely* rational does not do justice to the relationship. A relationship involves more than just the mind: it involves the heart, the soul, and every part of our being.

Love, like faith, is far greater and more all-encompassing than reason alone. In that sense, faith in God is rational, but also greater than reason itself. Pope John Paul II wrote:

> Faith and reason . . . each without the other is impoverished and enfeebled
> . . . Deprived of reason, faith has stressed feeling and experience, and so

runs the risk of no longer being a universal proposition. It is an illusion to think that faith, tied to weak reasoning, might be more penetrating; on the contrary, faith then runs the grave risk of withering into myth or superstition. By the same token, reason which is unrelated to an adult faith is not prompted to turn its gaze to the newness and radicality of being . . .

. . . Faith and reason are like two wings on which the human spirit rises in contemplation of the truth.[3]

Faith is never forced

Faith is like love. Love never coerces, and it is never forced. The knowledge of God is not forced upon people either, but is promised to those who seek

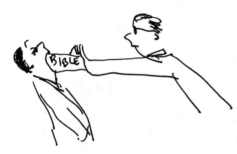

Him. Jesus said, "'Ask and it will be given to you; seek and you will find" (Matthew 7:7). The great French mathematical genius Blaise Pascal, who came to faith in Christ at the age of thirty-one, pointed out that God has provided enough evidence of Himself to convince those of us who have open hearts and minds, but this evidence will never convince those who are closed to the idea of God:

Willing to appear openly to those who seek Him with all their heart, and to be hidden from those who flee from Him with all their heart, God so regulates the knowledge of Himself that He has given indications of Himself which are visible to those who seek Him and not to those who do not seek Him. There is enough light for those to see who only desire to see, and enough obscurity for those who have a contrary disposition.[4]

So the answer to the question, "How much evidence is there?" is that there is not enough evidence to be coercive or to force belief, but there certainly is enough evidence to conclude that faith is by no means irrational. The writer of Hebrews defines faith by saying, "Faith is . . . the *evidence* of things not seen" (italics mine, Hebrews 11:1, KJV).

Faith in Christ is also part of a relationship

For a Christian, faith is not simply about believing in something, but about trusting someone. Faith is like love. It is not only a matter of "privately entertaining the opinion that a thing called 'God' exists."[5] Rather, faith is at the heart of a relationship—a relationship with a God who has made Himself known in Jesus Christ. That is why the analogies that the New Testament writers use to describe this relationship are the terms used to describe the closest personal relationship: the relationship between a parent and a child, or a husband and a wife. This relationship of trust transforms our lives, as well as all our other relationships.

All relationships involve an element of trust—not only a relationship with God. Pope John Paul II said, "There is no doubt that the capacity to entrust oneself and one's life to another person and the decision to do so are among the most significant and expressive human acts."[6]

A relationship with God is indeed a matter of faith, but not at all a faith against all the evidence. What is this evidence that we base our faith on? Let us explore some of the reasons why faith is credible and viable in the modern world, by looking at the evidence of God the Creator, the evidence of Jesus and the evidence of transformed human lives.

Evidence of God the creator

The apostle Paul made the assertion that, "Since the creation of the world God's invisible qualities—his eternal power and divine nature—have been clearly seen, being understood from what has been made" (Romans 1:20). He was clearly convinced of there being some sign or rumor of God in the creation itself. What is the evidence for this assertion?

Evidence from the fact that there is "something rather than nothing"

As we look at the world around us, it is natural to wonder why it is here, or where it came from. Modern science has actually sharpened that question for us. "The existence of the Big Bang begs the question of what came before that, and who or what was responsible."[7] This view is often unpopular. As Stephen Hawking has written, "Many people do not like the idea that time has a beginning, probably because it smacks of divine intervention."[8] Einstein was among those who developed this view. He initially tried to resist the implication

"maybe it was a balloon bursting"

of his theory of General Relativity (that the universe has a beginning) by trying to formulate a model reconciling the theory with a static universe. He finally abandoned the attempt and accepted that the universe did have a beginning and the implication of "the presence of a superior reasoning power," albeit while rejecting Judeo-Christian ideas of God.[9]

For many, this evidence points to the existence of God, but others (including Hawking himself) seek to provide alternative explanations. The question scientists attempt to answer is, "If the Big Bang is how the world started, what caused the Big Bang?" Did it come from nothing? Or, is it possible to suggest it was caused by God?

In the final paragraph of his book, *God and the Astronomers*, the astrophysicist Robert Jawstrow wrote:

> At this moment it seems as though science will never be able to raise the curtain on the mystery of creation . . . Now we see how the astronomical evidence leads to a biblical view of the origin of the world. The details differ, but the essential elements and the astronomical and biblical accounts of Genesis are the same; the chain of events leading to man commenced suddenly and sharply at a definite moment in time, in a flash of light and energy.[10]

Evidence from the "fine tuning" of the universe

As we touched on in Chapter 3, although their answers differ, scientists such as Stephen Hawking have at least shown that, "Even infinitesimally small differences in the original explosion that cosmologists see as the starting point of our universe would have resulted in a world where conscious life would not occur."[11] If anything, the weight of the evidence for the fine-tuning of our universe and our world is on the increase.

Professor Anthony Flew was one of the most influential rationalist atheist philosophers. But in 2004, he changed his mind. The *Church Times* said, "Flew . . . abandoned his life-long commitment to atheism and he now accepts that God exists. In his own words he 'simply had to go where the evidence leads' and recognize that 'the case for God is now much stronger than it was before.'"[12]

Evidence of the nature of human beings

The philosopher David Hume pointed out that you cannot derive an "ought" from an "is."[13] If things just are, as some atheists claim, then there cannot be absolute right and absolute wrong. But in that case, where does this innate sense of right and wrong that we all seem to carry within us—whether Christian, agnostic, or atheist—come from? Paul says that it is the way we are created. God made us with a conscience. He writes that the requirements of the law are written on our hearts. Sometimes they accuse and sometimes they defend us, because we have a conscience (Romans 2:15).

Another compelling piece of evidence to do with human nature is the longing that many find within themselves for something transcendent. St. Augustine (AD 354-430) said, "You formed us for yourself and our hearts are restless until they find their rest in you."[14] This is the evidence of experience, the emptiness that is in every human heart. Deep down we know that material things alone cannot satisfy, and that even human relationships are not enough. Bernard Levin, perhaps the greatest columnist of his generation (and who was not a Christian), seemed to be only too aware of the inadequate answers to the meaning of life. He wrote:

> Countries like ours are full of people who have all the material comforts they
> desire, together with such non-material blessings as a happy family, and yet
> lead lives of quiet, and at times noisy, desperation, understanding nothing
> but the fact that there is a hole inside them and that however much food
> and drink they pour into it, however many motor cars and television sets
> they stuff it with, however many well balanced children and loyal friends they
> parade around the edges of it . . . it aches.[15]

This is human experience. Even in a secular society such as Britain, around 70 percent of people claim to believe in God. How do we explain the fact that so many people in the world believe in God or are open to the possibility of God's existence? Many critics of religion suggest that people believe only because they were brought up that way. But, upbringing does not solve the question of why so many people believe.

A student once said to the great Archbishop of Canterbury William Temple, "You believe what you believe because of the way you were brought up." To which Temple replied, "That is as may be. But the fact remains that you believe that 'I believe what I believe because of the way I was brought up' because of the way you were brought up."

Many have also suggested that religion is wish fulfilment. Yet, as C. S. Lewis pointed out, "Such wish fulfilment would likely give rise to a very different kind of God than the one described in the Bible."[16] The God of holiness and justice, who calls His followers to costly obedience and discipleship, teaching love and forgiveness, even of enemies, is certainly not the wished-for God of all and sundry!

Of course, wishing for something does not guarantee the existence or non-existence of that something. When St. Augustine reflected on the God-shaped hole in every human heart, he was not suggesting that what is wished for must exist (though he certainly thinks it is a clue). Rather, St. Augustine is pointing us to look at the peace, rest, and joy that Christians testify to time and again in relationship with God.

Evidence of God the Liberator

People who profess Christian faith today can look not only to the evidence of creation and of human nature, but also to the historical life of Jesus Christ. John Stott has written:

> God is partly revealed in the ordered loveliness of the created universe. He is partly revealed in history and in experience, the human conscience, and the human consciousness . . . Nevertheless, God's full and final self-revelation . . . has been given in and through Jesus alone. . . . That is the reason why every enquiry into the truth of Christianity must begin with the historic Jesus.[17]

Evidence of the life of Jesus

No one seriously doubts the fact that there is a great deal of evidence for Jesus' existence. This comes not only from the Gospels and other Christian writings, but also from non-Christian sources. For example, the Roman historian Tacitus wrote that, "Christ, from whom they [Christians] got their name, suffered the extreme penalty [i.e., the crucifixion] during the reign of Tiberius at the hands of one of our procurators, Pontius Pilate."[18]

There is plenty of evidence both inside and outside the New Testament for the existence of Jesus.[19]

Evidence for the death and resurrection of Jesus

Jesus Christ's physical resurrection from the dead is the cornerstone of Christianity. For myself, it was through the life, death, and in particular the resurrection of Jesus that I came to believe that there is a God. Christians come to know who God is through these events of history into which God has entered. The world-renowned New Testament scholar Tom Wright said this:

> The Christian claim is not that Jesus is to be understood in terms of a God about whom we already know; it is this: the Resurrection of Jesus strongly suggests that the world has a Creator, and that that Creator is to be seen in terms of, through the lens of, Jesus.[20]

What is the evidence that the resurrection really happened? There are four historical facts in the Gospels that need to be examined:

- Jesus' burial
- The discovery of His empty tomb
- Eyewitness accounts of His post-mortem appearances
- The origin of the disciples' belief in His resurrection.

Tom Wright concludes his book *The Resurrection of the Son of God* by saying that we have to face two facts which, taken together, are extremely powerful:

> We are left with the secure historical conclusion: the tomb was empty, and various "meetings" took place not only between Jesus and his followers ... but also ... between Jesus and people who had not been his followers. I regard this conclusion as coming in the same sort of category, of historical probability so high as to be virtually certain, as the death of Augustus in AD 14 or the fall of Jerusalem in AD 70.[21]

Wright goes on to describe the explosion of Christianity that took place around the whole known world. He says, "That is why as an historian, I cannot explain the rise of early Christianity unless Jesus rose again, leaving an empty tomb behind him."[22]

Evidence of God the Transformer

For many people the most impressive evidence for the existence of God is the reality of transformed lives and transformed communities. The apostle Paul wrote, "We . . . are being transformed into his image with ever-increasing glory, which comes from the Lord, who is the Spirit" (2 Corinthians 3:18).

Evidence of the transformed lives of Paul and the apostles

There is a great deal of historical evidence that the apostles' lives were transformed by what they believed to be an experience of the risen Jesus Christ and the outpouring of the Holy Spirit. Let us consider one example.

With astonishing suddenness, Paul, who had been persecuting the church, became the leading advocate of Christianity. What caused this turnaround? Paul was quite clear in his answer, "Have I not seen Jesus our Lord?" (1 Corinthians 9:1). He lists the early appearances of Christ and then adds "last of all he appeared to me also" (1 Corinthians 15:8). The book of Acts corroborates Paul's claim to have seen the risen Jesus (Acts 9:4 ff; Acts 22:7 ff; Acts 26:14 ff).

In the eighteenth century, two eminent lawyers, both atheists, Lord Lyttleton and Gilbert West, were absolutely determined to destroy the Christian faith. They made an agreement between them that they would do this by undermining two things: the resurrection of Jesus Christ and the conversion of St. Paul.

In *Observations on the History and Evidences of the Resurrection of Jesus Christ*, Gilbert West set out to disprove Jesus' having risen from the dead. On the flyleaf of the book, West quoted Ecclesiasticus 11:7, "Do not find fault before you investigate." He sifted the evidence for the resurrection from a legal standpoint, and he finally become satisfied that Jesus was raised from the dead in the way the Gospels described.

Lord Lyttleton's book was entitled *Observations on the Conversion and Apostleship of St. Paul*. He also studied the evidence from a legal standpoint, and he became convinced that Saul of Tarsus was converted in just the way described in Acts, becoming a radically new man. In the course of writing his book, Lyttleton too experienced a conversion and became a Christian. Of the evidence for the transformed life of St. Paul, Lyttleton wrote, "The conversion and apostleship of St. Paul alone duly considered is in itself demonstration sufficient to prove Christianity to be a divine revelation."[23]

Evidence of transformed lives and communities

The countless examples of transformed lives in church history and of today offer further evidence of the rationality of faith. The conversion of St. Augustine, the conversion of Martin Luther and the conversion of John Wesley number among them. Personally, I have heard innumerable stories of people whose lives have been transformed by Alpha at our church and around the world. A typical conversation might go:

"Were you a Christian?"
"No I wasn't."
"What happened?"
"I encountered Jesus."
"What difference has Jesus made to your life?"
"Well, He has transformed my relationship with my wife."
or "Well, He's set me free from drug abuse."
or "He's set me free from alcohol abuse."

Francis Collins, former leader of the Human Genome Project, is one of today's leading scientists. He had been raised by freethinking parents and became first an agnostic and then an atheist. He worked in medicine and recounts what happened:

I was raised by . . . freethinking parents . . . for whom religion was just not very important. . . . I became first an agnostic and then an atheist . . . One afternoon, a kindly grandmother with only a few weeks to live shared her own faith in Jesus quite openly with me, and then asked, "Doctor, what do you believe?". . . I fled the room, having the disturbing sense that the atheist ice under my feet was cracking, though I wasn't quite sure why. And then suddenly the reason for my disquiet hit me: I was a scientist. I was supposed to make decisions based on evidence. And yet I had never really considered the evidence for and against faith. As I explored the evidence more deeply, all around me I began to see signposts to something outside of nature that could only be called God. I realized that the scientific methods can really only answer questions about HOW things work. It can't answer questions about WHY—and those are in fact the most important ones. Why is there something instead of nothing? Why does mathematics work so beautifully to describe nature? Why is the universe so precisely tuned to make life possible? Why do we humans have a universal sense of right and wrong and an urge to do right . . . Confronted with these revelations, I realized that my own assumption— that faith was the opposite of reason—was incorrect. I should have known better: Scripture defines faith as "the substance of things hoped for, the evidence of things not seen." Evidence! Simultaneously, I realized that atheism was in fact the least rational of all choices . . . How could I have had the arrogance to make such an assertion? After searching for two years more, I ultimately found my own answer—in the loving person of Jesus Christ. Here was a man unlike any other. He was humble and kindhearted. He reached out to those considered lowest in society. He made astounding statements about loving your enemies. And he promised something that no ordinary man should be able to promise—to forgive sins. On top of all that having assumed all my life that Jesus was just a myth, I was astounded to learn that the evidence for his historical existence was actually overwhelming. Eventually, I concluded the evidence demanded a verdict. In my 28th year, I could no longer deny my need for forgiveness and new life—and I gave in and became a follower of Jesus. He is now the rock upon which I stand, the source for me of ultimate love, peace, joy, and hope.[24]

Time after time after time, all around the world, millions of people are experiencing the risen Christ today. This is evidence. It is not just individual lives that have been transformed, but whole communities.

The church itself is evidence. The church has made a difference to the lives of billions of men and women. It has had an impact on society, on culture, on the arts, and on philosophy. It has had an impact on family life, on the dignity of human beings, on the rights of children, on care for the poor, for the sick, for the dying and the homeless.

Evidence of transformed understanding

C. S. Lewis said, "I believe in Christianity as I believe that the Sun has risen, not only because I see it, but because by it I see everything else."[25] Not only can you can see the rising sun, but by it you see everything else that is around you. Lewis's point was that coming to faith gives a whole new understanding of this world.

St. Anselm of Canterbury said, "*Credo ut intelligam*" (I believe in order that I might understand). This is very similar to the way that science works. First, you come up with a theory, and then you test it with the evidence. It is through belief that we come to understand the world—belief in Jesus, ". . . in whom are hidden all the treasures of wisdom and knowledge" (Colossians 2:3). Our understanding of the purpose of this universe comes through faith.

Faith is certainly not irrational. In fact, its relationship with reason is an ongoing process. In Pope John Paul II's book *Fides et Ratio* (*Faith and Reason*), following a chapter entitled "Credo ut Intelligam" (I believe in order that I might understand) there is a chapter entitled "Intelligo ut Credo" (I understand in order that I might believe). In other words, when you come to believe, you don't stop exploring.

Today's prevailing cultural attitude is to assume that Christians just stop thinking. This is simply not the case: when you become a Christian you become, if anything, *more* interested in everything. You start exploring God's universe. Reason, in the context of relationship, is given permission to question, to investigate, and to go on learning.

Two examples of how Christianity transforms our understanding of the world are the twin stories of creation and the fall. The doctrine of creation gives a context to the ubiquity of beauty—that there is something noble about every human being.

The doctrine of the fall explains why nothing is ever quite perfect —both in the created world and also in the human heart. Aleksandr Solzhenitsyn, the great Russian novelist, wrote, "The line separating good and evil passes not through states, nor between classes, nor between political parties either, but right through every human heart, and through all human hearts."[26]

This is the understanding that the Bible gives us in order to make sense of the world. Faith can make sense of religion, atheism, the human mind, the rational structure of the universe, justice, and friendship. Most of all, faith makes sense of love.

Perhaps love is the most powerful transfiguration of human understanding. If this world has no God, if it just came about, how do we explain love? British theologian Graham Tomlin writes of how the reality of love offers us two possibilities:

> At the end of the day there is a simple choice to be made. Is love a "misfiring instinct," an accidental by-product of evolution, and a thinly veiled strategy for personal or genetic survival? Or is it actually the centre of reality, the reason why we are here? For Christians, it is the very centre of all that we are. We are made in the image of a God who is love and we were made to learn to love and to be loved. That is the whole meaning of our existence. Christians suggest that we have a deep instinct that tells us that love is no accidental by-product, a "blessed mistake" but is in fact the very centre of the human experience of human life and happiness.[27]

Conclusion

I can only conclude with my own experience. I started out life as an atheist. When I was a teenager I argued against Christianity for a long time. I started to investigate further when two very good friends, Nicky and Sila Lee, told me that they had become Christians. I was concerned for them and this gave me an incentive to look into it.

I started to read the New Testament. I didn't read the Gospels as the inspired Word of God; I simply read them as historical documents. Yet, to me they had a ring of truth. I saw that there was evidence for Jesus and I had to make a choice. It certainly was not wish fulfilment because at that moment my thinking was that, if Christianity was true and if I was to become a Christian, life was going to be terrible! However, I thought that, if it was true, I had to become a Christian. So I said "yes," thinking that really was the end of all enjoyment of life.

The moment I made that step, I experienced the living Jesus Christ, the risen Jesus Christ, and I realized that this was what I had actually been searching for all my life without knowing it. I wasn't conscious of a God-shaped gap, but I was always searching for the next thing with which to try to satisfy it.

" I'd appreciate the
chance to stuff it with
cars, tv.s and children..

just to see ...."

When I experienced that relationship with God through Jesus Christ, my longing was satisfied. I experienced God's love for me through the Holy Spirit. It broke my belief that everything we do in life is selfish. I began to realize that, if there is a God, He can break through with His love and give us a freedom to love that makes such a difference to our lives. This is what I have experienced in the last forty years.

Life has not always been easy since then. There is the dark night of the soul, there are painful experiences of doubt and suffering, all kinds of things that challenge our faith, and more. But my experience has been that there really is good evidence for our faith. Our faith is not irrational; it is rational. It is also beyond rationality—it is relationship, relationship with the God who made us. For me, the key thing is to be able to say, along with the apostle Paul and along with countless others, "I know whom I have believed" (2 Timothy 1:12).

ENDNOTES

Chapter 1

1. John Stott, *The Cross of Christ* (IVP, 1986), p. 311.
2. C. S. Lewis, *The Problem of Pain* (Fount, 1940), p. 14.
3. *Ibid*, p. 59.
4. David Watson, *Fear No Evil* (Hodder & Stoughton, 1984), pp. 114-15.
5. *The Times* (October 19, 1991).
6. C. S. Lewis, *op cit*, pp. 81, 83.
7. Christopher Compston, *Recovering from Divorce* (Hodder & Stoughton, 1993), p. 142.
8. David Watson, *op cit*, pp. 119-20.
9. C. S. Lewis, *op cit*, pp. 30-31.
10. Alister McGrath, *Suffering* (Hodder & Stoughton, 1992), pp. 100-101.
11. Joni Eareckson and Joe Musser, *Joni* (Pickering & Inglis, 1976), p. 96.
12. John Stott, *The Cross of Christ* (IVP, 1986), pp. 336-37.

Chapter 2

1. Statistics from the 2011 UK Census, http://www.ons.gov.uk/ons/rel/census/2011-census/key-statistics-for-local-authorities-in-england-and-wales/rpt-religion.html
2. Statistics from the 2011 UK Census *op cit*, and the European Social Survey 2008.
3. Bernard Levin, *The Times* (January 27, 1992).
4. Stephen Neill, *The Supremacy of Jesus* (Hodder & Stoughton, 1984) p. 82.
5. John Stott, *The Contemporary Christian* (IVP, 1992), p. 308.
6. John Young, *The Case Against Christ* (Hodder & Stoughton, 1986).
7. Stephen Neill, *The Supremacy of Jesus* (Hodder & Stoughton, 1984), p. 82.
8. Lesslie Newbigin, *The Finality of Christ* (John Knox Press, 1969), p. 59.
9. Alister McGrath, *Bridgebuilding* (IVP, 1992), p. 151.
10. C. S. Lewis, *Mere Christianity* (Fount, 1952) p. 39.
11. J. N. D. Anderson, *Christianity and Comparative Religion* (IVP, 1970), p. 105
12. John Stott, *op cit*, p. 319.
13. Lesslie Newbigin, *op cit*, p. 59.
14. Michael Green, *Evangelism Through the Local Church* (Hodder & Stoughton, 1990) p. 75.

Chapter 3

1. *Time*, God Vs. Science, November 5, 2006.
2. Richard Dawkins, *The God Delusion*, (Black Swan, 2006), p. 189.
3. C. S. Lewis, *Miracles* (Fontana, 1947) p. 110.
4. John Polkinghorne, *One World* (SPCK, 1986), p. 1.
5. Cited in William Oddie (ed.), *After the Deluge* (SPCK, 1987), p. 118.
6. John MacMurray, *Reason and Emotion* (Faber, 1961), p. 172.
7. http://articles.latimes.com/2009/nov/24/opinion/la-oe-masci24-2009nov24
8. John Polkinghorne, *The Daily Telegraph* (August 24, 1992).
9. CNN, "Collins: Why this scientist believes in God", April 6, 2007. http://edition.cnn.com/2007/US/04/03/collins.commentary/index.html
10. The term "miracle" is sometimes used very loosely to describe, for example, remarkable answers to prayer. It is helpful to distinguish "providence," i.e., the guiding or steering by God of nature, humankind and history, from a "miracle," which has been well-defined by David Atkinson (*The Wings of Refuge* (IVP, 1983), p. 13) as a "non-repeatable, counter-instance of an otherwise demonstrable law of nature," e.g., walking on water, raising the dead or multiplying food.
11. David Hume, *On Miracles* (1748), p. 114.
12. Max Planck, *A Scientific Autobiography* (Williams and Norgate, 1950), p. 155.
13. C. S. Lewis, *Miracles* (Fontana, 1947), p. 51.
14. John Stott, *Essentials* (Hodder & Stoughton, 1988), p. 221.
15. Dr James Moore has pointed out that, contrary to popular belief, it was not the theologians who opposed Darwin as much as the scientists. "It was few theologians and many scientists who dismissed Darwinism and evolution" (Michael Poole, *Science and Belief*, Lion, 1990, p. 102).
16. Stephen Hawking, *Black Holes and Baby Universes and Other Essays* (Bantam Press, 1993).
17. Charles Darwin, cited in Francis S. Collins, *The Language of God: A Scientist Presents Evidence for Belief* (Simon & Schuster, 2007), p. 99.
18. British physicist Paul Davies, author of *God and the New Physics* and other works, is one of the most popular science writers today. He is notably unsympathetic to conventional Christianity.
19. John Polkingthorne, *One World* (SPCK, 1986), p. 57.
20. Stephen Hawking, *op cit.*
21. J. B. Phillips, *Gathered Gold* (Evangelical Press, 1984).
22. *The Times*, April 10, 1993.

Chapter 4

1. European Commission, *Social Values, Science and Technology Report*, 2005: http://ec.europa.eu/public_opinion/archives/ebs/ebs_225_report_en.pdf

2. Statistics from the US Census 2008: http://www.census.gov/compendia/statab/2012/tables/12s0075.pdf

3. Caryl Matrisciana, *Gods of the New Age* (Marshall Pickering, 1985), p. 15.

4. *New York Mag*, "Our Lady of Malawi," May 1, 2011: http://nymag.com/print/?/news/features/madonna-malawi-2011-5/

5. John Stott, "Conflicting Gospels," *CEN* (December 8, 1989), p. 6.

6. Eckhart Tolle, *The Power of Now: A Guide to Spiritual Enlightenment* (Hodder, 2001).

7. Caryl Matrisciana, *op cit*, p. 81.

8. John W. Travis and Regina Sara Ryan, *Wellness Workbook*, 3rd edition (Ten Speed Press, 2004), p. 258.

9. Russell Brand, *The Guardian*, "Big Brother isn't watching you," August 11, 2011.

10. David Icke, *The Truth Vibrations* (The Aquarian Press, HarperCollins, 1991) p. 20.

11. See http://www.oprah.com/omagazine/A-New-Earth-What-I-Know-for-Sure-by-Oprah-Winfrey

12. Shirley Maclaine, *Going Within* (Bantam Press, 1989), p. 30.

13. *Ibid.*, pp. 180–81.

14. David Icke, *op cit*, pp. 115–17.

15. Foundation for Inner Peace, *A Course in Miracles* (Penguin, 1975).

16. Michael Green, *The Dawn of the New Age* (Darton, Longman & Todd Ltd, 1993), p. 86.

17. Caryl Matrisciana, *op cit*, p. 220.

Chapter 5

1. Tobias Jones, "Secular fundamentalists are the new totalitarians," *The Guardian*, January 6, 2007.

2. Francis Collins, *The Language of God*, (Simon & Schuster, 2007), p. 231.

3. Thomas Paine, *Age of Reason* (1795), quoted in Brian McLaren, *Everything Must Change* (Nelson Books, 2008), p. 157.

4. Dawkins writes that, "DNA neither cares nor knows. DNA just is. And we dance to its music." In Richard Dawkins, *River Out of Eden: A Darwinian View of Life* (Phoenix, 1996), p. 155.

5. Rod Liddle, *Sunday Times*, October 8, 2006.

6. John Brockman, *What is Your Dangerous Idea? Today's Leading Thinkers on the Unthinkable* (Simon & Schuster, 2006) p. 300.

7. Christopher Hitchens, *Letters to a Young Contrarian* (Basic Books, 2005), p. 55.

8. Paul Copan, "Jesus, Religions and Just War" (Ravi Zacharias International Ministries USA, 2007) http://www.everystudent.com/wires/justwar.html

9. John Lennox, *Gunning for God: A Critique of the New Atheism* (Lion, 2011), pp. 64–65.

10. John Humphrys, *In God We Doubt* (Hodder, 2008), p. 184.

11. Keith Ward, *Is Religion Dangerous?* (Lion, 2006), p. 74.

12. John Humphrys, *op cit.*, p. 293.

13. John Cornwell, *Darwin's Angel* (Profile Books, 2008), p. 90.

14. Michael Bourdeaux, *Patriarch and Prophets: Persecution of the Russian Orthodox Church* (Mowbrays, 1975), p. 38.

15. "Christianity's Cultural Contributions: Rob Moll interviews Jonathan Hill," *Christianity Today*, March 2006.

16. David Bentley Hart, *Atheist Delusions: The Christian Revolution and Its Fashionable Enemies* (Yale University Press, 2009), p. 31.

17. John Humphrys, *op cit*, pp. 217, 232, 322.

18. Charlie Mackesy, from a talk given at HTB, London, January 6, 2008.

Chapter 6

1. The Athanasian Creed is a widely accepted statement of what Christians believe, which emphasizes ideas about Jesus, and about the Trinity.

2. J. I. Packer, *Knowing God* (Hodder & Stoughton, 1973), pp. 68–70.

3. John Stott, *God's New Society* (IVP, 1979), p. 52. (Now reissued in the series *The Bible Speaks Today*.)

4. *Ibid*, p. 191.

5. *Ibid*, p. 207.

6. J. N. D. Kelly, *Early Christian Doctrines* (Adam and Charles Black, 1960), p. 229.

7. Gerald Bray, *Creeds, Councils & Christ* (IVP, 1984), p. 178.

8. *The Times*, June 25, 1992.

9. *The Times*, July 1, 1992.

10. *Ibid*.

11. John Eddison, *Talking to Children* (H. E. Walter Ltd, 1979), p. 15.

12. Alister McGrath, *Understanding the Trinity* (Kingsway Publications, 1987).

13. *Ibid*, pp. 138–139.

14. *Ibid*.

15. C. S. Lewis, *Mere Christianity* (Fount, 1952), pp. 138–39.

16. Alister McGrath, *op cit*, pp. 136–37.

Chapter 7

1. The conversation is reported in John Dominic Crossan, *The Dark Interval: Towards a Theology of Story* (Argus Communications, 1975), p. 31.

2. *The Times*, October 9, 2007, p. 55.

3. John Paul II, *Fides et Ratio -Encyclical Letter of Pope John Paul II* (Catholic Truth Society, 1998), p. 3.

4. Blaise Pascal, *The Pensées: Thoughts, Letters and Minor Works*, Section VII, 430.

5. Quoted in Lash, "Where Does The God Delusion Come From?," *New Blackfriars Magazine*, p. 512.

6. John Paul II, *op cit*, p. 50.

7. Francis Collins, *The Language of God*, (Simon & Schuster, 2007) p. 66.

8. Stephen Hawking *A Brief History of Time From the Big Bang to Black Holes* (Bantam Press, 1988) p. 46.

9. Hugh Ross, *The Fingerprint of God* (Promise Publications, 1991), page number unknown.

10 Robert Jawstrow, *God and the Astronomers* (W. W. Norton, 1992), pp. 107,14.

11. Stephen Hawking *A Brief History of Time From the Big Bang to Black Holes* (Bantam Press, 1988) p. 46.

12. Paul Badman, *Church Times* (October 26, 2007).

13. David Hume, 1738, reference unknown.

14. St. Augustine, Confessions, Book 1, Section 1.

15. By kind permission of Bernard Levin.

16. Francis Collins, *op cit*, p. 37.

17. John Stott, *Authentic Christianity*, (Inter-Varsity Press, 1996), p. 47.

18. The Roman historian Tacitus, concerning the "Great Fire of Rome" in *Annals*, Book 15, Chapter 44 (c. 116).

19. For a more in-depth discussion on the historical evidence for Jesus' existence please see "Who is Jesus?" and "Why Did Jesus Die?" in Nicky Gumbel, *Questions of Life* (Alpha International, 2010).

20. N. T. Wright, *The Resurrection of the Son of God* (Fortress Press, 2003), p. 170.

21. *Ibid.*

22. N. T. Wright, "The New Unimproved Jesus," *Christianity Today*, September 13, 1993.

23. Lord Lyttleton, *Observations of the Conversion and Apostleship of St. Paul* (1747).

24. Remarks delivered by Francis S. Collins at the 55th Annual Prayer Breakfast, February 1, 2007 in Washington DC, USA.

25. C. S. Lewis, *The Weight of Glory: And Other Addresses* (HarperCollins, 2001), p. 140.

26. Aleksandr Solzhenitsyn, *The Gulag Archipelago 1918-1956* (1973).

27. Graham Tomlin, "Dawkins—A Theologian's Perspective" in Nicky Gumbel, *Is God a Delusion?* (Alpha International, 2008), p. 108.

FOR FURTHER READING

Chapter 1
Pete Greig, *God on Mute* (Kingsway, 2007).
C. S. Lewis, *The Problem of Pain* (Fount, 1940).
Jane Oundjian, *Facing Bereavement* (Alpha International, 2005).
John Stott, *The Cross of Christ* (IVP, 1986), especially chapter 13.
David Watson, *Fear No Evil* (Hodder & Stoughton, 1984).
Philip Yancey, *Where is God When it Hurts?* (Zondervan, 1997).

Chapter 2
Nicky Gumbel, *Questions of Life*, (Alpha International, 2010), especially the chapters "Who is Jesus?" and "How and Why Should We Tell Others?"
Stephen Neill, *The Supremacy of Jesus* (Hodder & Stoughton, 1984).
Lesslie Newbigin, *The Gospel in a Pluralist Society* (SPCK, 1989).
John Stott, *The Contemporary Christian* (IVP, 1992), chapter 18.

Chapter 3
Francis Collins, *The Language of God: A Scientist Presents Evidence for Belief* (Pocket Books, 2007).
Roger Forster and Paul Marston, *Reason and Faith* (Monarch, 1989).
Alister McGrath, *Surprised by Meaning: Science, Faith and How We Make Sense of Things* (Westminster/John Knox Press, 2011).
John Polkinghorne, *One World* (SPCK, 1986).

Chapter 6
Alister McGrath, *Understanding the Trinity* (Kingsway Publications, 1987).

Chapter 7
Richard Bauckham, *Jesus and the Eyewitnesses* (William B. Eerdmans, 2008).
William Lane Craig, *Reasonable Faith* (Crossway, 2008).
Tim Keller, *The Reason for God* (Hodder & Stoughton, 2009).
Amy Orr-Ewing, *But is it Real?* (IVP, 2008) and *Why Trust the Bible?* (IVP, 2008).

what is alpha?

Alpha is a practical introduction to the teachings of Jesus Christ that gives guests an opportunity to explore the meaning of life. The 10-week course is presented free of charge in a relaxed, friendly setting featuring good food and easy conversation.

Alpha is for everyone, welcoming people from all backgrounds, religions and viewpoints. It covers crucial topics like: the existence of God, the purpose of life, and the teachings of Jesus.

find out more
alphausa.org/whatisalpha

word on the street

》 "Over the course my desires started to change. I don't touch drugs now...I don't know what I would have done without God in my life." – James

》 "There were no phonies or holier-than-thou attitudes. No question was treated as stupid or irrelevant. It was a safe place to explore and learn." – Matt

alpha stats

world
169 countries
22.5 million guests
81 languages

usa
50 states
3 million guests
127 denominations

what happens at alpha?

The Alpha Course usually lasts for 10 weeks with a day or weekend getaway in the middle. Courses vary in size from one small group meeting in a home to hundreds of people in a church and can be run at any time of day. The talks each week cover the following topics, acting as a springboard for the small group discussions.

alpha course topics

Introduction Dinner .... Is there more to life than this?
Session 1 .... Who is Jesus?
Session 2 .... Why did Jesus die?
Session 3 .... How can we have faith?
Session 4 .... Why and how do I pray?
Session 5 .... Why and how should I read the Bible?
Session 6 .... How does God guide us?
Weekend/Day Away .... Who is the Holy Spirit?
What does the Holy Spirit do?
How can I be filled with the Holy Spirit?
How can I make the most of the rest of my life?
Session 7 .... How can I resist evil?
Session 8 .... Why and how should we tell others?
Session 9 .... Does God heal today?
Session 10 .... What about the Church?

typical course

• 45 minutes – Food, Drink and Conversation
• 45 minutes – The Talk (DVD or Live)
• 1 Hour Small Group Discussion
The Alpha course is FREE of charge to guests.

find an alpha course

Find a course near you and attend by looking on the website of your country that can be found on the contact page (pg. 121).
Please know you are welcome there!

Let's connect
Would you like stay up to date on all God is doing through Alpha in transforming lives, communities, and churches? Join our mailing list and share your Alpha experience. As a token of our appreciation, you can choose a free gift. You can also find other ways to get involved, like becoming an Alpha Advisor, joining a Global Alpha Team and many more.
www.alphausa.org/connect
Or call us at 800.362.5742

Tell us your story
Has your life been changed in an Alpha Course? We would love to hear how God worked in your life. It might be just what someone considering attending an Alpha Course needs to hear to take that next step.
www.alphausa.org/mystory; www.alphacanada.org/stories

Go deeper in the Word
Looking to strengthen your faith journey? Subscribe to Nicky & Pippa Gumbel's "Bible in One Year Plan." Receive a daily email devotional that coordinates with the Bible in One Year Reading Plan.
www.alphausa.org/bibleinoneyear
www.alphacanada.org/bibleinoneyear
www.alpha.org/bioy (Caribbean and Latin America)

Join our online communities
Looking for like-minded people who are talking about their recent experience in Alpha? Join the conversation on social media.
Facebook - Alpha USA; Alpha Canada; Alpha Caribbean; Alpha Latin America
Twitter - @alphausa; @alphalatam; @alphacanada
Alpha Friends - alphafriends.ning.com

getting started with alpha

STEP 1
prepare for
your course

We're here to help you with your preparation
Regional Alpha offices are located across the country and are eager
to help you get your Alpha Course started. Contact us to connect
with a network of experienced Alpha coaches and churches in your
local region.

STEP 2
plan
your course

Planning a successful course is simple
Alpha hosts training events and conferences across the country
providing you and your volunteers all the training you need to run
the course. Topics include: Hosting Small Groups, Pastoral Care,
Praying for Others on Alpha, and more. These topics and many other
training resources are available (in print and video) in our store –
alpharesources.org

STEP 3
promote
your course

Promoting your course is easy with our helpful tools
Empower your church members and friends to catch the vision to
invite their unchurched friends, neighbors, co-workers and family.
From invitations, to videos and suggested timelines, the Alpha
website is full of creative promo ideas.

BEGIN
start your
journey

Connect with us to begin your Alpha journey
It's time to get started impacting lives through Alpha. We're here to
help you. Contact us today!

Refer to our contact information on the last page for your country.

**Alpha provides a wholistic approach for ministry, equipping
churches to transform their communities.
We offer resources for:**

Evangelism

Discipleship

Family Life

alpha's offerings

Evangelism

JUST CURIOUS KIT

For anyone interested in running an Alpha Course or presenting the idea to others. Includes 1 of each of the following: *Questions of Life* book; *The Alpha Course Manual*; *How to Run the Alpha Course: Telling Others* book; *Why Jesus?* booklet; *Alpha Course Introductory* DVD, *What Is Alpha* promotional brochure and a copy of *Alpha News*. 83378

30 DAYS

An excellent introduction to Bible reading designed to be read over thirty days. Nicky Gumbel has selected thirty passages from the Old and New Testaments which he has found particularly helpful. It is designed to complement the talk "Why and How Should I Read the Bible?" on the Alpha Course and is also ideal for others who are interested in beginning to explore the Bible. 54058 / 978 1 938328 20 6

QUESTIONS OF LIFE
(also in eBook)

Questions of Life is the Alpha talks in book form. A great read for an Alpha Course attendee or for someone just beginning their journey of discovery.

Packed with humor, anecdotes, wisdom, and profound teaching from the Bible, Nicky Gumbel introduces the person of Jesus Christ and invites the reader into a world of discovery that has fascinated human beings for 2,000 years. Questions of Life has now been completely updated and revised. 105021 / 978 1 934564 06 6

THE ALPHA COURSE DVD FULL LENGTH AND EXPRESS VERSIONS

These DVD sets comprise the 15 talks for the Alpha Course. The full length version includes the complete talks, whereas the express version contains talks that have been shortened to between 20-25 minutes in length. *Alpha Express* is ideal for use in the workplace or in other contexts where there may be less than an hour to run the course. 15153 / 15154

THE ALPHA COURSE GUEST MANUAL

This newly designed manual is a "must have" for all guests on the Alpha Course, as well as for hosts and helpers. This essential resource is now even more appealing for guests and its new design makes it easier to use. The manual contains newly revised content and has a fresh and contemporary feel. 15204B / 978 1 934564 58 5

Discipleship

THE JESUS LIFESTYLE BOX SET
A study based on the Sermon on the Mount.
25328

A LIFE WORTH LIVING BOX SET
A study based on the book of Philippians.
71258

THE JESUS LIFESTYLE
(also in eBook)

Our culture is obsessed with lifestyle. Magazines and websites tell us what to wear, how to get fit, what to drive, and how to love. Everyone wants to tell us how to live our lives.

Jesus didn't leave us a lifestyle magazine. He sat down on a mountainside and began to teach. 25327 / 978 1 934564 48 6

A LIFE WORTH LIVING

A nine-session course based on the book of Philippians. This course is aimed specifically at those starting out in the Christian life and is ideal for those who have just completed an Alpha Course. Each talk explains how it is possible to live the Christian life positively, practically, and joyfully. It covers such topics as "New Attitude," "New Friendships," and "New Responsibilities." 71257 / 978 1 934564 08 0

FAITH IN A CHANGING WORLD
BY LESSLIE NEWBIGIN

With a new introduction by leading Newbigin scholar, Paul Weston, this book brings together two of Newbigin's classic works: *Discovering Truth in a Changing World* and *Living Hope in a Changing World*. Together, they present the Christian story as a lens through which to view and understand God and the world, demonstrating that Christianity is a viable way to live one's life today, and that Christians need not retreat to a private world where faith is presumed to be "mere opinion." 180354 / 978 1 907950 35 3

CAFÉ THEOLOGY
BY MICHAEL LLOYD

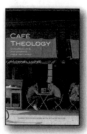

In Café Theology, Mike Lloyd invites us to grab a cappuccino and travel with him from Creation to New Creation. Whether we've been on the Christian journey our whole life, we're just starting out, or we haven't even bought a ticket, this extraordinary book is applicable to our ordinary lives. Updated with helpful index.

54053 / 978 1 905887 90 3

relationship central

THE MARRIAGE PREPARATION COURSE

STARTER KIT

Everything you need to start a course for 5 couples:

1   Leaders' Toolkit
1   Course DVD Set
2   The Marriage Book
1   Leader's Guide
10 Course Manual
Promotional Material
100718

SAMPLER
101724

THE MARRIAGE COURSE

HOME STUDY BOX SET

Want to do the course with you and your spouse or with a couple of friends or neighbors? Here is a kit designed with you in mind.

Includes 1 Marriage Course DVD, 1 Marriage Book, 2 Marriage workbooks, and some training help to show you how it is done.
102735 / 978 1 934564 24 0

SAMPLER
102724

THE MARRIAGE BOOK

This best-selling book by Nicky and Sila Lee is essential reading for any married or engaged couple.
102726 / 978 1 934564 65 3

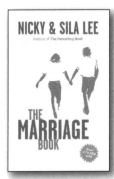

THE PARENTING CHILDREN COURSE

HOME STUDY BOX SET

Includes: book, DVD, discussion guide, parent guide (2), course overview booklet
100912 / 978 1 933114 83 5

SAMPLER

100928

THE PARENTING TEENAGERS COURSE

HOME STUDY BOX SET

Includes: book, DVD, discussion guide, parent guide (2), course overview booklet
100913 / 978 1 933114 87 3

SAMPLER

100929

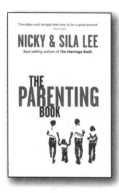

THE PARENTING BOOK
BY NICKY AND SILA LEE

Drawing on personal experience, Nicky and Sila Lee bring fresh insights and time-tested values to the task of parenting. Full of valuable advice and practical tips, *The Parenting Book* is a resource for parents to come back to again and again.

100900 / 978 1 934564 51 6

If you are interested in finding out more about Alpha please contact:

Alpha U.S.A.
2275 Half Day Road
Suite 185
Deerfield, IL 60015
Tel: 800.362.5742
Tel: + 212.406.5269
e-mail: info@alphausa.org
www.alphausa.org
www.alpharesources.org

Alpha in the Caribbean
Holy Trinity Brompton
Brompton Road
London SW7 1JA UK
Tel: +44 (0) 845.644.7544
e-mail: americas@alpha.org
www.alpha.org
Web: Caribbean.Alpha.org
FB: Alpha In The Caribbean
Twitter: @AlphaCaribbean

Alpha Canada
Suite #230 – 11331 Coppersmith Way
Riverside Business Park
Richmond, BC V7A 5J9
Tel: 800.743.0899
Fax: 604.271.6124
e-mail: office@alphacanada.org
www.alphacanada.org

To purchase resources in Canada:

David C. Cook Distribution Canada
P.O. Box 98, 55 Woodslee Avenue
Paris, ON N3L 3E5
Tel: 800.263.2664
Fax: 800.461.8575
e-mail: custserve@davidccook.ca
www.davidccook.ca

Alpha

Available wherever Christian books are sold.